DISCOVER THE OFF-GRID PROTOCOL

Spines

DISCOVER THE OFF-GRID PROTOCOL

AN EASIER WAY OF GOING OFF-GRID...

TARVIN DURBIN

CONTENTS

CHAPTER 1
INTRODUCTION / OFF-GRID: WHO'S IT FOR?

There are a lot of people in the world today who are growing ever so tired of living in the everyday Rat-Race and dealing with all of the different self-imposed problems that our society is gradually forcing us to live with. These people do not agree with how the world is rapidly changing and have had their eyes opened in many different ways over the past few years by the unwanted changes and newly fabricated rules that are continually being imposed upon them. They have a hunger to do their own thing, and this particular group of people is unique in its own way and doesn't want to follow the crowd. They are continually looking for different ways to detach themselves and their families from all of the unsettling craziness that is growing around them. This group of people is in search of a more peaceful and simpler lifestyle, and for the most part, they just want to be left alone. This group of people has started saving their money, working on gathering up their resources, cashing in on their retirement funds, educating themselves about off-grid living, buying suitable land, building an off-grid home, water collection, solar power, homesteading, gardening, canning, raising chickens, raising ducks, raising goats and other livestock, prepping, survivalism and just about anything that has to do with being self-sustainable in some form or another and they are constantly doing research on how they can make this all become a possibility for themselves.

Some people want a change in their lifestyle so badly that they will do just about anything to achieve their goals. As you well know, there is a ton of information out there. In fact, there is so much information that it can be overwhelming and hard to know where to begin. You may start off making different lists and asking yourself... Where do I go? What do I buy? What do I need? Etc. So again, you end up asking yourself... What is Real? Where do I Start? and how do I get to where I want to go from here?

One of the things I have noticed the most over the years is that many people have a misconception about Off-Grid living. They think that if you move off-grid, you're going to have to lower your standard of living and live in a small shack or dirt hut. This is simply not true. The beautiful thing about building and living off the grid is that you're in charge of your quality of living. You're in charge of the outcome of your project. You can design and build your very own Off-Grid Hideaway however you wish. I would first suggest that you start out with a small budget and build what you can afford as you go. Now, of course, if you have the money and resources available to you, then you can make your build come together much faster. My point here is that... that part is totally up to you. The biggest thing I would like to emphasize here is that you are the common denominator here, and you should take your time, do your research, make your list, make your comparisons, and then go over all the options that are available to you before you start the project. Once you can do these things, then sit down and start putting together your plan. Do whatever you can to make it fun.

I know that some people can be a little nit-picky and even a little critical or harsh to judge how we often do things sometimes, and with that being said... I would like to add my own little disclaimer, so to speak. While this book is not designed to be a Step-By-Step or How-Too Book, I am writing this book as a preliminary guide of sorts to help give you some insights about a lot of different things that you may or may not be aware of and that you should consider in order to help you to determine whether you feel that building your own off-grid style home is right for you or not. Now, I will tell you that there are harder ways to build off-grid, as well as easier ways to build off-grid. Some of those ways will require more hands-on labor and resources, as others may require more money to accomplish certain tasks. I am also not saying that this is the only way, and maybe not even the best way of doing some things. However, this is how I like to do things based on my own research and past experiences. I hope that you will find what I'm going to share with you to be informative and that it will also motivate you to press forward with your dreams and goals of moving off-grid and building your own small off-grid home... My recommendation for you, once you have finished this book, is to do even more research on this subject because the more you can learn on this topic, the more knowledgeable you will become and the more it is going to clarify what you need to do and what steps you need to take to reach your objective... My thought is that even if you only take one thing away from reading this book that can help you move forward in your journey, it is all worth it in the long run. Remember, this is your journey. Your journey is different from mine. It is unique only to you. Remember your WHY... Find ways to make it enjoyable and find ways to make it fun. Celebrate your small victories, keep pressing forward and don't look back.

First and foremost, In my opinion. If you want to be away from the crowds and on your way to living a more carefree life with less stress and chaos in our world today, you need to have your own home. One of the things that people need most in the world today is housing. Everyone needs a warm, dry, safe, and secure place to lay their head. A place to call home. Yet, it's something that feels completely out of reach for so many people in our world today. Housing is actually a global issue; it's not just an issue here in the States. When it comes to housing, especially here in the States, having a home of your own can feel like an unattainable goal for so many people. Government rules, regulations, building codes, permitting, home inspections, giant mortgages and so on. It seems the list of roadblocks is almost never-ending. I guess that is true to some degree, depending on your financial status and where you are located. However, if you are willing to open your mind a little and do some research, you will find that there are still many areas out there where you can still buy affordable land that you can build your home on that doesn't have any building restrictions, permitting requirements or regulations for building. Yes, they can sometimes be hard to find. But the land is out there if you look hard enough. I guess it all basically comes down to just One Question... How bad do you want it? Followed by a few more... Are you willing to relocate? Do you have an open mind? Will you do what it takes to make your dreams and visions come true? Sometimes, it's about finding a loophole or a workaround, technicality and so on. I was introduced to Alternative Building back in 2001, which was several years ago, and I'll tell you that I have been hooked on the concept ever since. A lot of people who know me will sometimes roll their eyes, take a breath and say, "Oh No...Here he goes again... " I love the concept of alternative building and absolutely love talking about it whenever I get the chance. I'll also tell you that the Alternative Building Concept is definitely NOT for everyone. It takes a certain mindset to get past all of the programming that society has invoked on us throughout our lives. You have to be willing to take a chance. That means you may win, you may lose. Who knows? That part is solely left up to each individual and how far they are willing to push themselves to get to where they truly want to be. I have had many failures along my journey, but those failures only gave me the incentive to push harder so I could continue to grow and achieve those few successes in my life, and those successes, my friend, were totally worth every bit of it. So, with all that being said, I'm going to dive right into it.

Throughout the course of this book, I am going to give you some valuable insight on building three different types of Off-Grid Structures that would make really nice Small Off-Grid Homes, complete with the systems that will make them totally comfortable, livable, and functional for you, although each of these structures is very different in their construction methods, materials, etc. Each structure has different levels of difficulty in building, and each structure has different benefits. However, the same principles for all the systems and the finishing details still apply to complete each structure. As you continue to read through the chapters, this will become clearer to you. Most people today are accustomed to big houses and lots of space. Well, when you get right down to it, a big house, although it may be beautiful to look at, usually has a large mortgage attached to it; a big house also has a lot of Waste. It takes a lot of energy and resources to heat and cool the wasted space within the house that nobody is even using, and that is big money coming out of your pockets that could be going towards something else or fewer hours you would have to spend at work and doing something else you would rather be doing if you didn't have that large monthly mortgage to pay every month. OK, so enough of that. I would first like to introduce you to a simple concept. The concept I would like for you to follow is to figure out just how much space you actually would need and start off by building "a small room" at first, just to get you started. Now hear me out ... Perhaps begin with something that may be the size of a large master bedroom that you could use as a small kitchenette with a bed, just for starters... for example. Then, finish out this room, and you will be able to move out onto your land faster. Once you complete the first room, you will then be able to add another room, such as a bathroom. So, just adding one tiny section would already make it more convenient. This would then make your small home even more comfortable. Then add on another room, such as a kitchen and so on... and before you even realize it. You will be living in your very own nice, comfortable home. That is TOTALLY PAID FOR!! With NO Monthly Payments to worry about. With this concept, you pay as you go and build your home as you can afford it. Having no monthly mortgage or rent payment to worry about means you will now be able to put that money, you would have been wasting on the mortgage or rent into your own pockets and have extra money to invest into your home instead.

Before we get into the details of how to accomplish all of this. You're most likely asking yourself, who is this guy, and why should I listen to what he has to say? Please allow me to introduce myself. My name is Tarvin Durbin. I joined the military right out of high school. I got a lot of different types of training in the military during my enlistment. I was stationed in Germany right out of high school; I was in Operation Desert Storm as a soldier. I Was in Operation Iraqi Freedom at Camp Speicher, Iraq, as a Civilian. I Was in Operation Inherent Resolve at Camp Taji, Iraq, as a Civilian, as well as deployed to several other crap holes over the years. I got out of the military in 1992 and was in the Aerospace Industry for 38 years. I held just about every position that the aviation industry offered at one time or another throughout the years: aircraft mechanic, fuel technician, supervisor, inspector, planner, and scheduler. I have worked and traveled to many places throughout the United States as well as around the world during my career. Having this kind of career meant that I had to spend a lot of time away from home and away from my family over the years. Which I am sad to say came at a cost to all of us because I was seldom home for them. The longer I was in my job the more I began to really dislike what I was doing. The industry had started to change more and more over time. New rules, new policies, new restrictions, etc... etc. As time went on, it was becoming harder and harder to do my job. It didn't matter what company I worked for or where I went. The industry was changing everywhere. The industry was promoting people who had no business being in their positions but were chosen because they wouldn't say no to anything that the company told them to do, even when they knew how they were jerking us around was wrong.

Whenever I started off in my career, I absolutely loved my job and what I did for a living. I was very proud of the fact that I had such a unique and credible career. You might guess that with the way the industry was changing and all the time I had to be away from home and all the time traveling to other places that, it eventually started having an adverse effect on me to the point where I was just miserable most of the time. Unfortunately, as time passed, I started drinking to cope with things. Then, over time I drank a little more, then a little more than I should have sometimes while I was away. Long story short, it finally caught up with me one night, and I ended up going to jail for assault and a DUI. (I believe that it was that night that woke me up!)

I promise that I am getting to the point... This all explains what led me to make the decision to turned my life around. Now, the funny thing about that (well, it wasn't funny back then) was that I was out with some guys I worked with in Daytona Beach. We had all gone out partying after work one evening. However, we did have a designated driver for the night to drive us around and make sure we got back to the hotel safely. Let's just say that things didn't end up going as planned. Once we got back to the hotel, I was feeling sick and stayed down in the parking lot in the car with the back door open because I was feeling sick. I told the guys I would be up in a little bit after I started feeling better. So, the guys went up to the room, and I stayed down in the car. The next thing I remember is that there were lights flashing all around the parking lot and there was a police officer waking me up. Turns out that the maintenance guy from the hotel called the law and yes, you guessed it... That was not a good thing for me. I ended up having to do a sobriety test... which I failed miserably. With the lights flashing all around the hotel parking lot, the guys I was with came down to see what was going on and much to their surprise, it was all about me. The guy who was our designated driver and the one who was driving the car left the keys in the ignition so I could get my bag out of the truck whenever I came up to the room. So, with the keys being in the ignition and since I technically had access to them, I was arrested for DUI even though all of the guys vouched for me and said they would all write statements and swear that I wasn't driving the car. However, that didn't matter to the police officers. I think it might have had something to do with my having a California driver's license at the time, but that's just me. The police officers told all of the guys to go back up to their rooms and that if they didn't stop interfering they were going to be going to jail with me. That comment caused me to become uncooperative, thus belligerent, which made things worse. So, fast forward a bit. I was living in Southern California at the time, and after I got back home, I had to go through all kinds of legal issues. I had big fines to pay, took the alcohol classes, lost my license for six months, and I had to do 150 hours of community service time for my punishment. I know that this scenario about my past has nothing to do with building, but it was this downward spiral in my life that caused me to finally "Wake Up" and made me realize that there was definitely more to life than the horrible path I was headed down. This incident is what forced me to go down another road, and from that point forward, it ultimately allowed me to become a better person and have a much better outlook on life.

My ex-mother-in-law was living with me and my family at the time, and she went to church at a small local monastery that was only a couple of miles from our house. It turns out that one of the monks from the monastery had a business background and had heard of my misfortunate incident. He asked if I would mind coming over to the monastery to meet with him. I accepted and went over to talk with him. Little did I know that meeting with this man was going to literally change my life and put me on a totally new path that I could never have imagined. His name was Father Basil. Before becoming a monk, he was a businessman, and not just any businessman. He was one of 3 men who invented plasma cutting technology, and Fr. Basil, well, he was the guy who actually sold it to the Aerospace Industry! He sat down and talked with me for a while and told me that they were getting ready to start a major building project and asked if I would be interested in coming over to help them out. He knew of my background and had heard of my misfortunate incident and the trouble that I had gotten into. I never knew it, but he actually had something else in mind for me, which I had no clue about at the time. So, Father Basil offered to let me serve out my community service time with the church (which was 150 hours) in order to honor my punishment for my DUI incident. I agreed to come help out with whatever they needed, and it turns out that we all got along very well together, so they offered me a position as a maintenance man working around the monastery grounds until they were ready to start their big building project then we could go from there. Well, shortly after that, they pulled me into the office and offered me the position of project manager for their building project. I was speechless, but naturally, I accepted their offer, and we got started right away planning how everything was going to work. They briefed me on what their plans were for the building project, and we laid out a plan. They told me that we were going to build adobe dome buildings on the back side of the monastery property for all of the monks so they could each have their own private quarters. I was really surprised at what they wanted to build, but I also thought it was pretty cool because I had always liked the domes I'd seen in different places, and now I was actually going to get to build some for myself. I still remember the day they got the Engineering Drawings back. We all sat down and started finalizing the details of the project so we could get started as soon as possible.

Immediately after that, I found out that they had Father Basil and myself scheduled to go to visit The Cal-Earth Institute in Hesperia, CA, which was conveniently only about an hour away from the monastery. I had lived in that area for a couple of years and never even knew that school was there... Needless to say, whenever we pulled up and walked through the gates at the fence and walked into the compound, I was totally amazed at what I saw. I had never seen anything like it. There was actually a Mini Village that they had built at the school. We walked up to the office and met with Nader Khalili. He was an architect originally from Iran, and he used to design skyscrapers. He had moved to the States sometime before and started The Cal-Earth Institute and he taught people from all over the world about this new housing concept of building your own home or emergency shelter by mostly using the earth that was right under your feet. This was back in 2001 when Father Basil and I were trained on the Earthbag or Super Adobe method, which is referred to by Nader Khalili himself, as well as a few of his other instructors. I remember back then Cal-Earth had just begun construction on "Earth One" as they call it... and The Eco-Dome. A lot of time has passed since then, and both of those structures are finished. They are amazing displays to check out for yourself if you ever get the chance to visit The Cal-Earth Institute someday. I highly recommend visiting. I know that it's definitely a time I will never forget.

Nader Khalili was a great man and very knowledgeable. I used to love to listen to his talks and lectures. They were incredible. He was very soft-spoken but definitely always had everyone's attention. I was blown away by everything he had taught us. I didn't know it until later on, but he was also the one who originally drew up the plans for the Domes on our project. Turns out that we were the first ones in the state of California to have that dome design signed off to Code within the state of California, which was a very big deal. All in all, it was a really cool project to be involved with. During the time that I worked with the monastery on their Dome Building Project, I will have to say that being a part of that particular experience had such a huge impact on me. I will even go as far as to say that the experience of building those domes and seeing how people reacted as we showed them what we were doing was just amazing to me and still amazes me to this day. I will even have to go as far as to say that being a part of that building project changed me somehow. It definitely changed the way I look at certain things. I have never felt such gratitude or satisfaction at anything I have ever done since that building project and being able to interact with others as we would show them around and explain to them what we were doing and actually seeing and experiencing a dome being completed and knowing I was a part of that is still mind-blowing to me, even to this day. There is nothing like walking inside one of them once it is completed. The sound, as well as the feeling of piece you get while being inside a dome, is something that I can't explain. It's something that everyone needs to experience for themselves.

*Nadar Khalili and Myself at the Cal-Earth Institute, Hesperia, CA.
First Eco-Dome Project, Late 2001*

Whenever I was first introduced to this alternative lifestyle and a different way of building, I guess I realized back then that teaching people how to build these structures was going to be something that others would need to know how to do for themselves. The more time passes and the more that the world changes, it just confirms to me that not only knowing how to build your own Off-Grid Sustainable Home may not be enough, but it's also the largest factor in getting you started and on your land. There are other things that we can get into, as well. Like knowing how to make your Off-Grid Sustainable Home Complete, by knowing how to do your own Water Collection and Filtration System, Electricity with Solar and or Wind Power to be able to provide your own power and how to Heat and Cool your home so it stays comfortable for you inside while it's hot and humid outside or if it's Cold you can stay warm. A point I'd like to make is that just because you're living Off-Grid doesn't mean that you have to give up certain creature comforts and luxuries that you love having to make yourself comfortable...

Growing your own food, Raising your own small animals like Chickens for their eggs or meat... Or Ducks for their eggs. Yes, Ducks... Duck eggs are amazing, and they are twice as big as chicken eggs. Here's a fun fact. Depending on the breed of duck. Did you know that just one duck on the right diet can lay as many as 290 eggs per year? Crazy Huh. Maybe some rabbits. Rabbit meat is considered to be some of the healthiest meat out there. Here's another fun fact. Do you know that Rabbit meat can sell for as much as $10 per lb? Maybe that could become one of your income sources... Who knows? Also, maybe you could raise limited livestock, like goats for meat or milk, and so on. Learning more things about how to take better care of ourselves is becoming more important all the time.

The Off-Grid Sustainable Industry is definitely growing. People are finally waking up to the way the world is changing, and they are getting sick and tired of the way things are. They are also realizing that our government is not exactly out for our best interests. It is, in fact, the opposite. The Fact here is that we all work harder and harder these days, and it is becoming more and more difficult to pay our bills and just get by anymore.

We stay so busy with working and running to catch up with ourselves that we no longer have time for ourselves or even the little things that should be important to us, like spending quality time with our families, not being able to just take a day off for an event that just so happens to be in the middle of the week that we really would like to go to because our boss tells us we can't have time off because they are short staffed or that they just don't want to let you have time off.

We're running around so much trying to get caught up on things that we don't have time to eat a decent meal, or we're too tired to cook something, so we stop by the drive-thru, and we eat on the run. We're so busy and tired that we keep energy drinks, sodas or maybe even sweet, flavored coffee drinks to keep us going so we're not so tired all the time.

I have continued to study and practice alternative lifestyles and alternative methods of building throughout the years, ever since back in 2001, when I was part of the Monastery Project in Southern California. I love sharing my ideas and my passion with others who have the same desire to learn more about building these incredible alternative structures for themselves. It is amazing how many people around the world are beginning to take advantage of these methods and learning what they need to do to create better lives for themselves and their families.

CHAPTER 2

YOUR PLAN: FINDING LAND / SOME THINGS TO CONSIDER

So, you want to move off-grid to start a new life. Everyone has different reasons for wanting to leave the hustle and bustle of the city. It is important that you know Your "WHY?" Become clear on your vision before you start this journey. You may need to sit down and evaluate the main reason or reasons for wanting to do this. Ask Yourself: What's the big reason for wanting to move off-grid, and why is it important to me? What do I want to accomplish by moving off-grid? Am I ready to face the different challenges that I will encounter? How do I prepare for my big transition from where I am to where I want to be? These are all excellent questions to consider.

Helping you to figure out the answers to these questions and more is what I am hoping to help you to answer within this book so you can feel more at ease with yourself and to help you get started on your dreams of being able to move off-grid and build your own home, as well as having some piece of mind along the way. Uprooting yourself from your current situation and moving off-grid may seem like the best thing to do, or perhaps it is something that you've always wanted to do. There are a lot of things you will need to consider once you actually decide to do it for real. So, I decided to write this book as a guide so that I could share with you some insights into what building off-grid is about. This book is Not a Step-By-Step Manual but is designed to be more of an in-depth guide to help break down and explain most of the different things that are involved in off-grid building to give you a heads-up so you can truly get a clear picture of what's involved in building off-grid, so you can see if this lifestyle is right for you before just jumping right in without knowing what you may be up against. I would also like to add that... Yes, I am sure that there are many other people and many other "off-grid" experts out there who may have a totally different way of doing things differently as well as even better, and that is perfectly fine. This is just my take on how I have learned to do things and how I would do them.

Figuring out your plan can sometimes be a little overwhelming, and as I said earlier, everyone's reasons are different to some degree. So, let's get right into it, shall we? First and foremost, you need to know what your budget is going to be for getting started. This is extremely important because this is where you let yourself know if you are able to resource the funds you are going to need to either go all out on your new life change or if you are going to have to work everything you are going to need to do on a tight budget. I'm betting that you are probably going to fall into the second category. This book is mainly structured around this. Yes, there are people out there who can come up with the money to do whatever they pretty much want to do, but all in all, that is not usually the case in today's society. We all work hard for our money and always have to try to budget what we have the best way that we can. Sometimes, your money is not necessarily where you may need it to be. So, a great first question would be, What's my budget? How much money do I have to work with? How much land do I want to have as opposed to how much land do I actually need to get myself started and onto the land? This will tell you right up front what you will need to look at as far as the size of the land as well as the cost of it, what you need to be able to come up with for your land, and whether or not you will need to be able to save up and pay cash for it or if you will need to get creative to be able to finance your future piece of land. Do not let any of these factors discourage you because there are different ways of being able to obtain a piece of land for your new home.

The first suggestion that I will make is to see if you can find a small enough piece of land that you may be able to just pay cash for if you are able to go that route. Next, I would see if maybe you have any relatives or family that have a small section of land that you may either be able to work out some kind of terms for them to sell you the land or perhaps even use in order to build your small home on. I know that avenue is generally not the way most people would want to go or even have an option of doing, but it never hurts to ask, just in case you know someone who may have some land that isn't being used.

You may or may not have the option of going the regular financing route with the banks depending on whether your credit is good enough and if you have a fair down payment to put down on a piece of land, which I believe is generally going to be at least 20% of the total asking price. Another method that many people use, and one that I have used myself, is to find a piece of ground that may be sold using owner financing.

Sometimes, you can work out some pretty good terms with a landowner for just a small down payment and affordable monthly installments. I was actually working with a realtor a few years ago. She had found a 10-acre property that was about 12 miles out of town that had just come to the market and called to tell me about it. I wasn't sure if it was what I wanted, but she gave me the directions to where it was located, and I went out to look at it that evening. Whenever I got to the property, I found that it was actually just what I had been looking for, and the bonus was that it had an amazing view of the mountains on the back side of the property. I called her back the next day and told her that I liked it and to see if she could give me some more details on the property. She called me back about 2 hours later and said that they wanted $26,000 for it. She also said that the Owners would be willing to do the financing and told me about the terms they were asking for, but they wanted a large balloon payment at the end of the loan. I didn't really like the terms they were asking because they wanted a balloon payment at the end. So, I came back with a counteroffer of giving them $10,000 Down and dividing the remaining payments up over the next 36 months or 3 Years and had the realtor submit my offer. The next day, the realtor called me back, and she told me that they had accepted my offer. The following week, I had an appointment with the title company and went in to sign the contract. I made my payments through the title company, and there were no issues. I made some double payments on the property whenever I could and ended up paying the property off early. I paid it off in 18 Months / A year and a half... instead of it taking me three years to do so, and everyone was happy. This also allowed me to have extra money during that time to put towards working on the property for improvements that would have otherwise been used as payments during that remaining time period.

Sometimes, land can be hard to find depending on where you are in the world and where you want your property to be. You are generally not going to be able to find the kind of land you are going to need near a town or city that will allow you to build the type of home that you want to build, nor will they probably allow you to build the kind of home that you're going to want to build either. I find that sometimes it is best to have a few different ideas and be willing to compromise a little if it can help you get where you want to be. That's why it is usually always best to find a piece of property outside of the city and sometimes even way out far away from anything, that is, if you are willing to move far enough away from modern conveniences to be able to have the life you want to live. I must make a note here that you must also understand that in order to have the kind of life that you want or that is required to have an off-grid style homestead or even to be able to build certain or different types and styles of off-grid homes, that you may have to also be further out away from a town to be able to build what you want.

Once you find a piece of land for yourself, you will need to look at the layout of the property. Is it sloped? Does it look like it will have drainage whenever it rains? Does it look like it is in a floodplain or low area? Does it look like it may flood if you were to get some really heavy rains? If so, is there a higher spot on the property you could build your home on so it wouldn't get flooded in a heavy rainstorm, or would you have the means to build this area up to put your home or other building structures on so they will not get flooded during a bad storm? The same goes for putting in a small garden to grow your own food, so ask yourself if that area may be subject to flooding. If so, would you consider compromising and setting up a vertical-style garden or raised planter beds for now in order to still have a small garden? That way you could possibly build up this area with dirt over time and be able to put in a nice little greenhouse in the future. Take into account any trees that may be on the property. You wouldn't want to build in front of them if they were going to end up blocking the sun. You would want to orient your home so that you could have the sun shining in through the windows to help heat the house during the winter months, or perhaps you're thinking of not wanting the sun shining through the windows into the living room during the summer months that may make the house hotter.

Are there going to be prevailing winds coming in the direction that you want the windows and doors to face? This may cause you to turn the house in a different orientation to keep the winds from banging on the windows and doors. These are things you may want to consider when orienting your home on-site before you build. Maybe even take note of the area surrounding where you want to build your house. Is it in a good place that you could possibly channel water from the roof into a water tank for your rainwater collection system? These are just some things to take note of and consider because once your home is built, it will be too late to change things. Now that you have found your land, here are just a few more things you will need to know before buying your land. I would advise that you ask these questions about the land, as well… For example, does the land in this area have any type of building restrictions, covenants, or codes that would keep you from building the type of structure that you want to build there? Make sure the property has access and knows what the easements are so you will have the ability to access your property; sometimes owners will not disclose this upfront, but it is something that you will definitely need to have… Otherwise, how are you going to be able to get on and off your new property? In some cases, if it isn't obvious that you do have access to the land, such as a road, you will need to know this… I would even go one step further and find the local county office where the land is located and check with them just to be absolutely sure that the landowner didn't just tell you what you wanted to hear, just to sell you the land. This way, once you get your home built, you won't have any issues with the county in which you bought your land. There are still several places you can buy land these days that do not have building restrictions, covenants or codes that will allow you to build however you wish. I know that all of these things can possibly be somewhat overwhelming, but I believe that you should just be aware of all these different things to consider, as well as doing your own due diligence and verify things for yourself.

This is yet another great way, and one of my favorite methods for you to search and find all sorts of different types of land is to look online. There are several websites that people use all the time to find exactly the kind of land they are looking for, and most of those sites generally advertise for sale by owner land, no credit, and even bad credit sales at very reasonable prices. Now, some may not offer the lowest interest rates around, but the rates are still affordable enough to get you to the exact kind of land that you are looking for. So, to me personally... Getting a piece of land that I can buy without any hassles and with ease is totally worth it to get myself out on a piece of land so I can build my home and start a new life. Some of the websites that you can search are:

www.LandWatch.com, www.Landmodo.com,

www.AnchorLandCompany.com,

www.HemmingwayLandCompany.com,

www.DiscountLots.com,

www.NunnLandSales.com just to name a few and you can generally find land at a pretty reasonable price along with low down payments and affordable monthly payment options. I highly suggest that you check them out and see what you think. They may just have the piece of property that's just right for your situation.

Now, just to reconfirm and show you that you can still find a nice little piece of ground, there's something that I would first like to share with you that might also help shine some light on not giving up on your dreams, as well as not letting anyone stand in the way of your dreams. After purchasing those 10 acres of desert land, I told you about earlier and spending over three years working my tail off trying to make myself a nice little homestead, I pretty much had to turn around and give it all up. Things just weren't working out in my marriage, and I wasn't happy with where I saw my life was headed. Yes, I could have stayed married and kept the property, but what is the point of sacrificing everything you can whenever you know in the end it isn't going to end up being what you are trying to work for? Bottom line, I was just miserable, and I knew it wasn't going to change, so I gave it all up. I have always dreamed of buying some land for myself and building a small off-grid cabin someday. Whenever I had purchased the 10-acre property prior, I honestly thought that was going to be my spot... However, it ended up that it just wasn't meant to be. So, I sold the property, got divorced, bought myself a 27ft Camper and moved into an RV Park in order to save money and to continue looking for a piece of property. After moving myself into the RV Park, I continued to look for a property and about four months after I had moved into the RV Park, and looking non-stop, I found a 2-acre piece of property up in the New Mexico Mountains. I couldn't believe it. I immediately contacted the owners, got the location information, and went to look at it the next day. The property is not super-close by, but it was totally worth going to look at. I actually had to go look at the property twice in 2 days because I wasn't sure of the property boundaries or exactly where the property was located. Long story short, it was totally worth going to see it again. It has an amazing view, and a bonus that I wasn't expecting is that it already has power, water, and internet access at the property line if I wanted to hook it up. Unbelievable. Needless to say, I jumped on it and purchased it right away. I guess there is something to say about not quitting your dreams. If you're patient enough and continue your search, things will come together. You just have to be persistent and not give up. Fast forward about two months. It was a weekend, and I had decided to sleep in a little. So, after sleeping in, I decided that I was going to get up, have a cup of coffee, grab a shower, and start my day. Well, I got up and made my coffee, and as I was putting in the creamer, BAM!! I had the worst pain I had ever felt across my chest, and then both of my arms and hands went totally numb... I was freaking the hell out. Yes, you guessed it. I had a heart Attack. I'm like, are you Freakin kidding me?? Really? Me? Why? I still can't believe it happened; I'm still blown away. It took me a while to finally come to terms with what happened, and after I got out of the hospital, I figured I was just going to embrace this and look at it as a new chance in life. After doing tons of thinking and debating on what I should do, what do I want to do?, what can I do?, etc... I made a promise to myself that my dreams aren't just something that I want to do... THERE'S SOMETHING I NEED TO DO!!! Writing this book HAS to be done, and sharing this book and my knowledge HAS to be done because I know that there are people out there who are looking for different answers and don't have the slightest clue of where to even start, and I believe that it's up to me to share my knowledge with them and try to help them in any way I can. Only if I can help guide one person it will all be totally worth it to me.

So, coming up in the future, I will not only be creating further course content based on what I am laying out in this book but also asking you lots of questions about things that you may be interested in learning more about. This book... Insights to Off-Grid Building is going to become the framework for building on my new property and an example for Building Your Small Off-Grid Home / Cabin.

CHAPTER 3

DESIGNING YOUR HOME, OPTION ONE: EARTHBAG CONSTRUCTION / DECIDING WHAT TO BUILD ON MY LAND

In the last chapter we talked about finding your land and once you found your land, some things you needed to take into consideration, as well as what to look out for before purchasing the land and one of the biggest things for you to think about is how you should orient your home on the property due to water drainage from rains, prevailing winds, potential shade from any trees or excessive sunlight from the sun, because once it's there it's going to be too late to change it.

Alright, you have found your land. It is time to check out the property, walk around it, and observe its layout. Look at the overall landscaping as well as the layout of the land and start identifying some potential different factors that may be an issue for where you have decided may be a good spot to build your home. Look at the overall property and notice if it is on an incline or if it is flatter. Do you have a chance of severe rainstorms? Try to decide where the prevailing winds will be coming from because you may not want to have your windows and doors facing the direction strong winds may be coming from. Try to notice which direction the sun rises and sets and where the sun may be located during the hottest part of the day because you may not want the hot sun shining through the windows of your living room area, making your house even hotter. Are there trees on the property that could potentially block any sunlight that you may want to come into the windows, either making it cooler or hotter depending on the time of year and what you would prefer most or perhaps you may want to turn the orientation of the home so the sun may predominately shine on the side of the house rather on the front side? These are just a few of the things that you should take into account when deciding to lay out where you are going to build your small new home. Once you have a good idea of where you are going to potentially build your home, you will then need to take into account the natural landscaping on your property and figure out where the utilities are going to be located, such as where a good place for the plumbing to go into the house as well as where will the drain coming from the toilet go before you start the build.

Since you have walked around and studied the layout of your new property, it is now important that I reiterate that once you decide not only where your home is going to be located but also the orientation/direction of where the front side of the house is going to be facing as well as where the back of your home is going to be facing. I think that you should at least take some pictures and sketch out a rough draft of a floor plan onto a notebook pad so you will have a reference to refer back to later on, not to mention that sketching or drawing this out will help bring your project more to life.

OK, you're probably asking yourself at this point, What about the home itself? How can I imagine this all coming together if I don't know what my home is even going to look like? What materials am I going to use? Is it going to be difficult or expensive to build?

These are all very good questions, and we are about to get into the answers to this right now. So, yes. With everything that you have accomplished up to this point, I definitely believe it is now time to start thinking about the actual design and layout of the floor plan for your small new home.

There are many different kinds of structures out there that you can build on your land, depending on your overall budget or time constraints. Some are quicker and easier to build than others, and some are a lot cheaper but more labor-intensive to build than others; some are more energy efficient than others, some are more costly than others and so on. I would like to bring to light a few of these different building methods and types to your attention. I would also like to share what I like about each of them and share my opinions about each of them with you to give you some different things to consider when deciding what style of home you think might be the best fit for you as you begin your new journey in building your future new sustainable off-grid small home.

The Alternative Methods and Styles of the homes I am going to share with you are nothing new. Some of these methods and styles of homes have been around for centuries and have started gaining more and more popularity over the past ten years or so because of either a need to create certain structures because of environmental catastrophes like hurricanes and tsunamis in other cultures or merely a desire for people to get away from the crowded cities to begin new lifestyles simply because they either wanted or needed to change their lifestyles. I would also like to add that there are many different opinions out there concerning some of these types of building structures. These Alternative building methods and styles are not for everyone. Some people love them for so many different reasons, and some people dislike the look because they are simply not built in the conventional style of architecture that so many people are accustomed to today. So, let's dive in and see which style/method may be right for you.

Although there are many different building methods out there, there are Three Primary Building Methods/Styles I would like to share with you. These are going to be: Earthbag Construction, Aircrete Construction and Shed to Home Conversions.

The descriptions I'm about to give you will explain the concept for each method, but they will not be the full step-by-step build breakdowns for each type of structure because in order for you to fully understand and comprehend the process of actually building a structure from these building methods you are going to need further detailed instruction, such as Material Lists, Tool Lists, Diagrams, Drawings, Measurements, Etc. on everything that's involved in building each of these particular building structures. I will, however, review each method in a manner that allows you to grasp each concept clearly enough to be able to decide which one is the right fit for you.

The first building method I would like to go over is the first alternative style building method that I was introduced to back in the summer of 2001 when I went to work with the Monastery in Southern California. This method is called Earthbag Construction. As I explained earlier in this book, I touched base briefly on the course of events that led to me working with Earthbag Construction. We referred to it as Building with Super-Adobe, which was basically a soil-based adobe mix that was stabilized with cement to prevent the mix from eroding, breaking down or washing away during harsh rains and bad weather. This method was introduced to me by Iranian-born architect Nadar Khalili, who founded the Cal-Earth Institute in Hesperia, CA. When I was introduced to him, it was impressive to hear that he had actually attended a 1984 NASA Symposium where he had brainstormed with them about ways to build structures on the moon. Yes, that's right. I said, on the moon. Amazing right? I remember my first visit there as if it were yesterday. The first time I walked through those gates onto the school grounds, I was totally amazed by the different structures that I saw there. There were even pictures there of NASA having astronauts come to the school for training on how to build structures on the moon using natural materials. The monastery had sent one of the monks, Fr. Basil, and me there to undergo training to learn to build these unique structures, as we were going to begin building these kinds of structures back at the monastery compound. We were mostly trained by none other than Mr. Khalili himself, as he was working closely with the monastery to guide them along with their building project at the time. I will say that it was purely a joy and an honor to be learning these valuable skills from such a master. This was a very exciting time for me; it was definitely something new. A time I will never forget, as I believe it was the start of a journey that changed my way of thinking from then on out.

Earthbag building is unique to most other building technologies because it can be considered to be either insulative or thermal mass, depending on what the bags are filled with. Insulative will tend to isolate the interior from the outside air, and thermal mass will slowly transfer outside air temperature into the interior. This is important because having these different characteristics in a wall will greatly influence how comfortable, economical, and ecological any system can be.

Generally, People build with regular sandbags, even feedbags or ricebags. The ones we used were polypropylene bags that are said to be able to hold up better to the UV rays from the sun. There are also Open Mesh Bags, commonly used to package fruit. This mesh can also be purchased in rolls and used in a similar manner to polypropylene bags. This method is known as Hyper-Adobe, and itt was introduced by Brazilianengineer Fernando Pacheco. So, whether you go with individual bags, Super-Adobe, or Hyper-Adobe bags, which come in rolls and, once filled, end up looking like a long tube, which can be cut and trimmed to any size you like. In my opinion, it is just a matter of preference. They can be used to make both straight and vertical walls, or they can be stacked to make various dome or vault shapes, Earthbags can also be used underground for building things such as water tanks, root cellars and even basements under your small home. So, you might be starting to see that building with earthbags can be very versatile.

On a Side Note: Sandbags, Rice Bags, Super-Adobe Bags and Hyper-Adobe Bags are all fairly easy to find. You may also be able to find bags that had blemishes or ones that had printing errors on them that they would also consider selling at a discount to save yourself a little money. Just do a simple online search and you should be able to find just about any kind of Sandbag you are looking for, and in just about any size you could want to build with, as well.

Building with earthbags can be done very economically, as well. In most cases, the majority of the material you will be using to fill your earthbags will come straight from the job site, using the soil under your feet and just adding in a stabilizer such as clay, lime, or cement. Whenever selecting your build site and you are going to build with earthbags, it is important to know what kind of soil you have on the property so you will know what you are working with and so you will know if it has the correct amounts of soil, sand, and clay percentages you are going to need to make your earthbag mix with. Make Sense? In order to do this, you are going to need to conduct a "Jar Test", which is a simple way of determining the clay-to-sand ratio in a potential soil mix. You will need to get a couple of mason jars or even some large clear glass jam or jelly jars, which I have used on occasion. You will need to first make sure the jars are clean. Then, you will need to take a sample of dirt from a shovel. It must be soil you are using to fill earthbags, NO organic materials or topsoil, only regular dirt. (Organic matter and topsoils will not bond well together and will leave voids and cavities in your mix.) Now you will fill your jar halfway with dirt and the rest with clean water. Put the lid on tight and shake it up really well. Set it down and let it rest overnight or until the water is clear again on top. The Coarse Sands will sink to the bottom, then the Smaller Sands and finally, the Silt will be on the top. You are looking for distinctive layers; these layers will show you approximate ratios of the type of soil you have on your building site. To give you a rough estimate, a fine top layer of about one-third to one-quarter thickness of the entire contents can be considered a suitable soil mix. If there is little definition between the soils, such as all sand, no clay, or it's just one murky glob, you may want to adjust what you have by having some clay and coarse sand brought in so you can fine-tune your mix design. And, of course, you could also use a mixture of lime or cement to help as a stabilizer as well. Whenever we were building at the monastery, we mixed in cement with our soil, and it worked out great.

Whenever you get your percentages right, you will be ready to start mixing. Before you start mixing, you will need a few other items for the project, such as: Materials: Sandbags (individual bags or rolls) Cement, Leather Gloves, a Tamper, Barbed Wire, a Center Stake with a nail on top or small caster for a pivot, a length of small rope or dog chain, key chain rings, lime, wheelbarrow or mixer, shovel, hoe, pickax, empty coffee cans, buckets, and a water source of some kind.

Some of these items might seem strange to you, but I assure you that each one of these items serves a purpose in the project. A brief review of what needs to happen next is that you will need to clear and level the work site. Once you clear the worksite, you will need to mark out the area where you are going to build. For example, let's say that you are going to build a small 20ft round dome structure. First, you will need to go to the center of your cleared building area and drive the stake into the ground, then put the swivel caster on top of it. Attach a small length of rope or dog chain to the pivot and measure out 10ft. Once you've done that, put your key chain ring on the end measuring out 10ft. Extend the chain and put a stick, screwdriver, or piece of rebar through the key ring or loop. Walk in a circle and draw a line in the ground. This will mark the perimeter of your dome. Once your perimeter is marked, you will either need to do a cement foundation for the floor of your dome, or you will need to do a perimeter ring foundation for the sandbags to sit on top of to form your walls. If doing a ring foundation, dig this out about a foot deep all the way around. Once this is dug out, you will need to pour in 2 courses of bags with rock for your foundation base, or you could put in cheap concrete bags and stack like blocks till you have your two courses for the foundation and remember to put barbed wire between the rows. Now that the foundation is done,

Marking out the site, digging the foundation trench and setting in the foundation bags

(You will need to put in the form for the door. Once you get up a couple of feet with the bag rows, you will need to put in the form for the window, and all you are going to do is lay the bags until they come to the form, and you are going to terminate at the form and restart on the other side of the form. And you will continue to lay the walls until you are finished with the dome.)

First few layers of bags and setting in the Door and Window Forms

You can start lying on the walls. Extend the chain from the center pivot and set your bags to the edge of where the end of the keyring is. Do this all the way around the wall. Once you close in the first row, go around with your tamper and tamp all the bags until they are flat and even. Then put down a row of barbed wire all the way around this course and then start laying in more bags for another row to be completed by using the end of the chain where you put the bags aligned with the end of the chain... go all the way around and continue to repeat these steps until you get to the top of the dome. You will notice that as you go up with the chain, the walls will start coming in; this is what will make this structure into a dome.

You will decide where you want the electric outlets and light switch to be and mark them on the inside. You will need to figure out where the electricity is going to come into the house, where the breaker box will be, where the plumbing will come in, and where the drain from the toilet will come out of the house. These areas will need to be dug out, and the conduit, water lines, and toilet drain line will need to be run out from under the wall so they can be stubbed out and hooked up later (If you poured a cement slab before putting up the walls, you will need to put these utilities in prior to pouring the concrete for the slab) You will start installing the conduit and outlet boxes before putting on the inside plaster covering. Now that the Dome structure is up, it is time to take out the door and window forms and start the plastering process on the outside. You can install the door and window at this time, as well; just try to be cautious about getting plaster on them. This process will continue until the plastering and paint is finished. It will now be time to start completing some finish work by installing the electric wiring, outlet boxes, light switches, lighting fixtures and covers. This will complete the electrical work inside the home. I will be covering hooking up power to the home in another chapter, where I'll discuss Installing the Solar System. The same will be done with the plumbing inside the house. Everything will be connected on the inside, such as the kitchen sink, kitchen sink drain, bathroom sink, bathroom sink drain, shower and shower drain, and toilet and toilet drain. These will all be running and stubbed outside of the house. This will be discussed in another chapter, where I'll discuss connecting the plumbing to the water pump and hooking up the drains to the DIY Septic System.

Roughed in Water Lines, Plumbing Drains and Electrical Boxes

You should be able to find everything at a number of places, such as Harbor Freight, Lowes Hardware, Home Depot, Tractor Supply, and any other Farm Supply Store. Amazon is also a good place if you'd rather just order online. But Try shopping around for the best prices first. Just keep in mind that there are many different ways to fill your sandbags.

*A Key Point I'd like to make about filling bags: Whenever filling the bags, make sure that you are filling them on the spot where you want to put the bag, this way you won't have to lift a full bag and move it every time you fill a sandbag. It will already be in place. Depending on the size of the sandbag you are working with, they can sometimes weigh as much as 50 to 100 pounds. It can get very tiring to have to move everyone to their place, so try to work smarter, not harder. Building with earthbags is very versatile. These bags can be used as the primary building structure entirely, or they can also be used as "fill in" as in using the bags to fill the wall voids between posts and studs in post and beam building or perhaps as using the bags to fill in the walls of a pole barn, as well.

The Walls are coming Up and Closing in on the Top of the Dome

I have tried to cover a lot on this building method without making it too complicated. As I said earlier, this is just a brief rundown covering Earthbag Construction to give you an idea of what is actually involved in building one of these structures. It might seem as if there is a lot to it, and maybe there is, but the big takeaway from this is that although this method may seem like a lot of work, it is one of the only methods that has been around for centuries and is still one of the cheapest ways to build with today. The main drawback for me is that there is a lot of labor involved. It does take some planning to make it all run smoothly, and it would be easier if you could get some volunteer help with a project. There are many good books and reference materials to review on the topic of building with earthbag construction. Here are a few of my favorite reads if you would like to learn more about this amazing yet low-cost way of building different structures. Building with Earth: A Guide to Flexible-Form Earthbag Construction, Earthbag Building: The Tools, Tricks and Techniques, Earthbag Architecture: Building Your Dream with Bags.

Outside Plaster Coat Going On... It's starting to look More Complete

If you decide to follow through with this idea, this is where your home will begin to start to become more visual to you. Now, think back a bit earlier and remember the stakes where you marked out where your home was going to be? Walk around this area again and begin to think things through; sketch out a drawing on your notepad of what this would look like sitting here in front of you, what value it would add to your property and what value it would add to your life. You should start visualizing your home sitting here, in all its beauty. Imagine yourself already moved into it and how your life has changed because of it. It's your dream. Live it!!

Earthbag Dome Plaster Coat, Finish Color and Trim Colors Complete

CHAPTER 4

DESIGNING YOUR HOME, OPTION TWO: BUILDING WITH AIRCRETE / DECIDING WHAT TO BUILD ON MY LAND

In the last chapter, we discussed building your home using Earthbag Construction. That particular method has been around for centuries. As with anything, there are many people who absolutely love to build using the Earth Bag Method, and there are also others who do not like this particular style of building because of the amount of labor that is involved in building structures using this method. Also, in the last chapter, I touched base on some different things for you to look out for, as well as some different things for you to take into consideration. Such as the slope of your land, where the water will drain off or pool up on your property. Which direction will the sun rise and set on your property, prevailing winds, etc. Many different things you should also consider when looking at the layout of where you are going to build your home or put your home on your land.

The next style of building that I would like to bring to your attention is Building with Aircrete. Although Aircrete is a different style of building, a lot of the same principles will still apply concerning the construction process. Aircrete has gained a lot of popularity over the past few years, but it is also new enough that a lot of people still have not yet heard of it. Aircrete, or Cellular Concrete has actually been around for many years, and it has actually been used as a building material in Europe for quite some time. However, in Europe, where they have primarily been building with cellular cement, the commercial side of it has also made its way into the United States. Large corporations invest a lot of money into the setup and manufacturing of cellular cement, which means that it is primarily produced in large factories using expensive, large, heavy, specialty equipment to produce commercial-grade cellular cement. It is only in the past few years that DIY Aircrete has come to be known in the United States. I remember first hearing about DIY Aircrete a few years ago. I was doing some research and came across an architect who had started making DIY Aircrete in Thailand he had developed his own simple, easy method for making DIY Aircrete using some basic equipment that he had built himself. I believe this was to be the turning point in making and building DIY Aircrete that we have come to know today thanks to the internet. DIY Aircrete is a homemade version of the commercial version of cellular cement, which is used in alternative buildings; however, since it is homemade by individuals and not made in a large commercial plant, it is not recognized as being the same thing. So, the government does not recognize it. The government's failure to recognize homemade DIY Aircrete as a suitable building material keeps a lot of people from pursuing their dreams of wanting to build with it. However, if you're dead set on going after your dreams and willing to do whatever it takes to make those dreams happen, you'll find ways to go around those who will do their best to try and stop you from making your dreams come true... So, if you are wondering if you can get a permit to build your home from your local county or city permitting office, the answer will most probably be "No," and with that being said, you will also not be able to get any type of conventional financing from any banks or lending institutions, as well due to the fact that DIY

Aircrete is considered to be an alternative style of building. You may be able to find some private investors that will be willing to finance your building; however, the interest rate will probably be high, and you will most likely have to own your land free and clear in order for the private investor to give you a loan. Depending on the state you want to build in, some county municipalities will allow you to build a structure that is 400 square feet and under or as a non-occupied structure and will give you approval to build a structure that may not require you to have a permit to build.

It is important to understand that because you have decided to take the steps necessary to move off-grid in order for you to have the freedom and independence that you're searching for, it is sometimes going to be necessary for you to come up with different solutions that will allow you to figure out different alternatives in order to circumvent some of the "rules" that our government entities have put in place over the years that they will say are put in place for your own safety. Yes, to a degree, this may have some truth to it, but overall, it only has to do with control and money. I would like to state that this, of course, is only my opinion, but nonetheless, it is what it is. I believe that once you start breaking away from the busy cities and begin your true adventure, you will begin noticing some things to be different than you actually perceived them to be prior to beginning your journey to move off-grid.

Perhaps here's something you could consider as an alternative to building your small home that may be an easier solution if you're having issues with your county municipality. If you are finding it difficult to gain approval for what you want to build, maybe consider changing the type of structure you want to build. How about thinking up a design for a cabin you can build using post and beam construction with a bond beam that will hold a conventional roof? Something similar to a Pole Barn Style

Framework. This sometimes makes getting a permit easier, as the Aircrete would then only be used as "in-fill" insulation, and you would still gain all the benefits of having an Aircrete Home without having to go through all the other hassles you might otherwise have to deal with trying to get a permit and building approval from a city or county municipality. I'm sure that if you were to do some more research, there may indeed be other avenues you could pursue in order to reach your building objectives. The method of using Aircrete as "in-fill" material in a post and beam structure is just one way that I found interesting.

In my opinion, Aircrete has many advantages and benefits depending on the application. My favorite thing to start off with is that it is lightweight to work with and definitely easy on your back, and if you can lift 20 pounds, you can climb a ladder. You are already able to be on your way to start building your own Small, Off-Grid Self-Sustainable Aircrete Home... Here are some other benefits that I would like to add as well, just to share some other added positives in working with this great material. It is inexpensive to produce compared to other materials; it has good compressive strength, it bonds well, it's easy to work with, it's easy to cut and trim with just simple hand tools, it's self-compacting, self-leveling, it uses less material because it is inflated, offers enhanced sound characteristics within its structures, it has great cooling and heating insulative properties, it is mold resistant, fire-proof, rot-proof, bug-proof and so on. One thing that I would also like to add as a small word of caution is that although Aircrete is a really great material to build with, it is still a brittle mix overall once it is dry. So, it is recommended that a thin, hard topcoat mix, such as stucco or an acrylic base concrete mix, along with a reinforcing fabric be applied as a final surface coat to make it solid and to keep it from chipping off easily. The way you make Aircrete is that you would generally use about 6 gallons of water to 94 lbs. of Portland cement mixed into a slurry. I like to use either a 55-gallon plastic barrel or a 55-gallon metal drum to make my Aircrete. I would then use a separate container, such as a 32-gallon plastic trash can, to mix up my soap solution. Add five additional gallons of water into the trash can, with 4 to 5 ounces of Drexel foaming agent that is made for creating the foaming solution. The Soap / Foam Solution is then pumped through a "Foam Machine" along with compressed air, which blends the soap/foam solution and air together to create a foam density that weighs as close to 95 grams per liter as you can get it. The foam is then pumped into the cement slurry mixture in the 55-gallon mixing barrel or drum. The batch is then mixed until it is inflated to about six times its original volume, which in turn is approximately 40 to 50 gallons of Aircrete mixture. You may be asking yourself. Where can I find a foam machine to make Aircrete with? Plans to build a foam machine can be found on the internet from several different places. A foam machine is fairly inexpensive to build, and you can pretty much purchase everything you need to build one from Amazon or your local hardware store. If you would rather purchase a foam machine instead of building one for yourself, you can just do an online search for Aircrete Foam Machines, and you will be able to locate a source to purchase from and have it delivered to your front door.

Aircrete Blocks can be made into many Shapes Building a Dome with Aircrete Blocks

Now, whether you are going to be building yourself a Dome, Cylinder-Style with a more conventional-style roof (similar to a yurt-style look), or a more traditional-style rectangular-looking home, As mentioned before, you will need to add in a layer of reinforcing fabric as well as a thin stucco or harder acrylic-based cement mix to help in making the surface stronger on the exterior walls as you build your home. This added layer of reinforcing fabric will tie everything together and help the wall, as well as the entire structure, become more monolithic in nature, and it will become stronger as well, and since Aircrete is predominately a softer, more insulative material for the most part and by adding in that layer of reinforcement fabric, topped off with a thin layer of acrylic based waterproof stucco or something similar your exterior walls will not only be strong, but solid and virtually maintenance free for years to come. If you want to build yourself a dome structure, you are going to have to make yourself a large form, which you will fill with the Aircrete mixture; then, once the mixture is dry, you will make blocks. You will need to allow them to cure and dry, and then those blocks will be used to build your dome structure. If building a more cylindrical structure that has more of the shape of a yurt, per se. It can be built by using a cast-in-place method that is accomplished by using an in-place form system, and then you can just continue building your walls by moving the molds up on the wall, further and further, with each course you pour. A Cement Bond Beam with rebar installed for additional strength around the middle of the bond beam would then be poured on the top of the uppermost row. This, in turn, will give the roof you choose to install a solid monolithic surface to rest on, as well as a strong place to secure the roof beams and rafters once the roof is ready to be installed. Now, with that being said. If you were building a more natural structure, the same method would still apply. The only difference would be the shape of the forms in which you are going to be pouring your Aircrete mixture. The Cement Bond Beam Section with a rebar added for additional strength at the top of your walls would be completed just as you did for the round, cast-in-place structure.

Different Dome Design Ideas with Unique Entrances

The interior will be much easier to finish and can be covered with something, such as a natural plaster or just simply be painted to your particular taste to complete. Conventional construction today is around an average of about $250 per square foot and up. Which can break the bank with about any budget, but you can build yourself a "Basic Shell" structure with Aircrete, for approximately $10 to $15 per square foot and you can "Finish Out" your small home, Complete with Doors, Windows, Kitchen with Cabinets, Sink and Countertop, Appliances, Bathroom with

Vanity, Sink Toilet and Shower. Ready to move in for around $50 per square foot, depending on what kind of furnishings and appliances you insist on having in your home... But for this price, even if you were to go all out and buy the nicer things to make your home really nice and cozy, you're still going to come in WAY Under what a "conventional build" would be today. Not to mention, with the money you are saving in the long run, you will be able to totally pay for your home and furnishings as you go while building and be debt-free with NO Mortgage payment when you are finished. Think back to the last chapter whenever I was talking about building your home by designing it so you could start off your build with just one main room and then add on another room as you needed it or while you were saving the money up and building on to your home after you had saved enough money. Allow your home to be built as you are able to build, free of stress and worry, instead of having to take out a loan and stay in debt.

Aircrete Pueblo Style Home Idea Small Modern Aircrete Home Concept Idea

Knowing that you are no longer going to be obligated to make a payment to the bank every month. Let yourself daydream a little now and think of how your days would be, knowing that your home was paid for, and you could focus your extra time as well as the extra money you are going to be saving and by being able to do other things you've always wanted to do and knowing you didn't have to go to work to make your house payment, that the extra money you were saving could go towards other things that could make an even bigger impact on the changes you could now start making in your life for you, as well as for your family. As I said earlier. Make a list of things that you want to do. Allow yourself to dream a little. Make this list of some of your new goals. Take pictures of your accomplishments. Start off with doing simple things you want to accomplish first. This will give you the ability to get some WINS under your belt. Once you are able to do these little things, then move on to larger goals and objectives... Then, soon enough, you will be able to look back on the accomplishments you have made and see how far you have come since you started out on your new journey. Yes, this may seem like a silly little task, but believe me, it may be simple, but it also works.

I have done this for a long time... I start with a small list of objectives, and whenever I accomplish all or even most of them, I always make another list for myself. This has always helped me to focus on the different things I need to get done so I am not so easily distracted and get off topic. Again, it is a simple little exercise, but it has always helped me to continue to move forward.

CHAPTER 5

DESIGNING YOUR HOME, OPTION THREE: SHED TO HOME CONVERSION / DECIDING WHAT TO BUILD ON MY LAND

In this chapter, the third type of small home I am going to cover is a Shed to Home Conversion. Converting a shed into a small home is something that a lot of people have done, and it is totally possible to do. Depending on the route you decide to take, it is a good way to help fast-track getting your property set up quicker as well as it can be more affordable, as well. It just depends on what your goals are and what your financial situation is. The beauty part about this method is that your small new home shell, at a minimum, will come "dried in," that means you can pretty much take the time you need to finish out the inside the way you want, as you are able to afford it. Without having to rush on your build and worry about the weather ruining your structure. Which makes this totally doable once you have your building in place.

These structures have become very popular over the past several years. People have many different reasons for their own individual builds, just as your reasons will most likely differ from a majority of people who want to build these types of homes. So, why build your small home out of a shed? Perhaps you are short on time, and you work a full-time job. Maybe having extra time to build your small home isn't a luxury you have at the moment, and you need something that you can move into right away, as opposed to having to wait several weeks or even months it might take you to resource all the materials you are going to need in order to build your small home, or maybe you live in an area that has a difficult climate to work in. Turning a shed into a small home would definitely cut down on your building time, which would allow you to move onto your land and into your home sooner than if you are going to build it from scratch by yourself. Plus, depending on what your skill level may be, if you are not familiar with the building process, doing a shed-to-home conversion would save you from possibly making costly mistakes or having setbacks in your project that you may not be counting on simply because you might not have ever done anything like this before.

Another reason might be that you may be able to buy a suitable shed for less money than you would be able to buy or build a small home shell for. Manufacturers have pretty much got shed building down to an art, and their processes are becoming more streamlined and efficient all the time, as well as they are most likely able to buy their materials in bulk and at wholesale prices, meaning that you should be able to pick up a higher quality product from them much faster and for less money than you are putting in the time and extra cost to build it yourself.

Either one of these would make Excellent Starter Homes, and could fit about any budget

I'm not saying that you can't build a shed to convert to a small home yourself, but unless you have a lot of experience with construction, any quality shed you buy is likely to be a higher quality candidate to become your small home than a small shell for a home that you could build yourself. By shopping around for different shed builders and reading their reviews, and seeing what some of their past customers have to say, it may be worth paying a little extra for the peace of mind that will come from knowing that your small home shell was built by pros who do it every day and that you won't have to worry about all the details or if maybe there might be something that you could be forgetting. On top of that, if you're building the shell for your small home yourself and something breaks or you build something wrong, you will only have yourself to blame. However, if you buy a pre-made shell from a manufacturer and something isn't right, your building should have at least some kind of limited guarantee once you make your purchase. Which should also help give you some peace of mind to some degree in case something goes wrong down the road.

When it comes to purchasing a shed from a manufacturer, most shed manufacturers today offer some kind of financing option. Depending on your situation and your needs, sometimes it's not a bad thing to look into their financing options. They may surprise you and possibly be able to accommodate something that just might fit your budget. If you have the option, I will try to compare some prices as well as their payment options before just accepting the first one that I find. As I'm sure, you are well aware of, when it comes to finances, Absolutely Everyone's situation is definitely different, which can sometimes cause us to have to scratch our heads and do some thinking in order to come up with some very creative ways to try and figure out how to be able to get what we want, or if this may even be an option for you. As you may know, it's sometimes hard to get financing for projects and things that most people are familiar with. A bank will be perfectly happy to put you into some deep debt in order for you to buy an expensive home however, when it comes to something that's unconventional, such as building, let's say, an Earthbag Structure, an Aircrete Structure or even a Shed to Home Conversion, they are most likely going to be reluctant on giving you any funds for any of these projects mainly because these kinds of projects aren't in the "Norm" of how things work in today's society. Not to mention, if you were only to borrow, let's say... $15,000 to build your own small home, they definitely wouldn't be able to lock you down in their 20-year and 30-year conventional style mortgages, and they would definitely be losing money in the long run. To me, it's the same as if you wanted to go buy a car. You only wanted to buy a car that was practical for your needs and for your budget, and it was something that you would be able to pay off relatively quickly. They are less likely to give you the loan to buy that vehicle because they are not going to make enough on it to make it worth their time. They'll say that it is too old, or it has too many miles on it, or your credit score isn't high enough or whatever any other excuse they like to use to be able to decline you for the vehicle loan.

What a difference a nice wrap-around porch and some stonework can do

I had this happen to me on a few different occasions. One occasion in particular was when I was getting ready to go contracting in aviation, as I had done for many years. I had bought myself a 5th-Wheel Camper and was going to use it for my housing while I was working and contracting over the road. I found a Ford F-350 4-door dual with a diesel engine, and it was a fleet truck that was traded in by another business because they had upgraded to a newer model truck. Anyway, this truck was absolutely perfect for what I was going to do. So, I went down to the dealership and looked at the truck, test-drove it and decided it was exactly what I needed and that it was also practical for what I needed it for. The price of it was a whopping $11,995. So, yes, it was perfect for me… But NO BANK would give me a loan because it was too old too many miles, my credit score wasn't where it needed to be, and my credit score was at a 720 at the time… I was pissed that I couldn't get the loan and that the only way I would be able to buy it was to pay cash for the truck. I asked the finance person, who in the hell has $12,000 just laying around? I told him if I had that kind of money, I wouldn't be here talking to him. I do believe I was just a little Irater than that at the time though… Now, here's the kicker, the same finance guy told me that he believed that he remembered a couple of other vehicles that they just got in that he thought would be a good fit for me based on what I was qualified for. So, he called the salesman to come back to the finance office and for him to take me back outside and show me the two other trucks that they had "Just got in" One was a newer model Chevrolet with only 300 miles on it for, get this, $52,000 and a newer model Dodge Platinum Dually Diesel with around 12,000 miles on it for $64,995. I was so mad and upset because all they cared about was getting me into debt. It still upsets me just to think about it. The saddest part of all is that people like this do this to unsuspecting people every single day and don't lose a second's sleep over it. Something I learned the hard way over the years is that you have to know what your budget is before you go looking at something, and if the deal doesn't feel right to you or you have any doubt or second thoughts... turn around and walk away. That's not to say that you shouldn't try to work out a deal with something that you are interested in buying. It just has to be affordable for you and fit within your budget. For example, if you are in the position of needing a shed or building that you want to convert into a small home for yourself just so you can get yourself started on the land and work towards your goals and dreams. If you can afford the payments, you are okay with whatever the interest rate might be, and it's going to eventually help you reach your goals and dreams. If you are comfortable with those terms, then I would say to move forward and get yourself started. But on the other hand, if you don't think that now is the right time, then wait. Look around some more. Save some more money to put down, make a plan, and set up a deadline. Anything that you can do that's going to help you reach your goals and dreams. It's certainly worth researching your options to see what's out there. You will just have to decide what is right for you, then make your decision and don't look back.

Once you decide on what you're going to do to get started on your journey, there are a few things that you should realize that may make all the work you're about to do totally worth it. 1st Off, Because a shed only costs a fraction of the price that a full-sized home goes for, you will be able to start living debt-free and mortgage-free much sooner because your bills will be lower, and you will start having more disposable income that will help you become more sustainable and to be able to gain more freedom to do more of the things you want to do in your life. 2nd, because your home is smaller, it will take less to heat and cool. However, if you were to set your small home up to be Off-Grid, you will not have any power or utility bills to worry about. To me, that is definitely something exciting to think about, and 3rd, Since your small home has a lower value, that means you will pay less in taxes because the amount of tax you pay is assessed according to the value of your property. Yet, another added benefit is that it will save you money in the long run.

Another Example of what a Nice Porch can do for your Shed to Home Conversion

With all that being said, let's move on to some of the things that you're going to need to consider when converting a shed to a small home. Off the top of my head, I can think of at least 10 different things that you'll need to start off with.

The first thing you would need to do before your small home gets delivered would be to at least scrape the surface and put down between about 4 to 6 inches of ¾" size gravel. Have your gravel base extend about 1 to 2 feet in all directions past where the edge of your home will be set. Then, make sure that the surface is level and well-compacted. You can do this with a small plate compactor to make this part go faster and easier. I know that most tool rental places will usually have this on hand that you can rent for the day and shouldn't cost much and will definitely be worth it in the long run. While you are putting in your base mix and packing it down, now would be a good time to think about any drainage that may flow either towards or around your small home. You may want to consider putting in a French Drain if you believe that there might be a possibility of any water being pushed towards your small home in a bad storm. Also, look at how and where any water might drain off your roof. You may need to put up some gutters and downspouts to help divert water that may come off the roof away from the pad area where your small home might be sitting to prevent having a muddy mess on your hands after a big rainstorm. However, since we are discussing Small Off-Grid Homes, I would suggest that you put up some gutters and divert the rainwater into a Water Storage Tank, IBC Tote, or 55 Gallon Plastic Barrels so you will be able to harvest the water for your reserves instead of just

letting all that precious liquid gold go to waste. This water can then be used for bathing, cooking, drinking, gardening and so on.

After thinking about this issue and deciding which avenue you are going to take, you will then want to think about how you are going to make the utility connections to your small off-grid home. I would just decide where you are going to put your utility connections at this time and not actually run them or connect them to your home at this time, as I would advise you that you should at least wait until the inspector has come and gone. That is, if you are going to connect to conventional utilities. Again, we are talking more about making your Small Home, Off-Grid... So, you should be thinking about installing your solar system and where you want your power source to be. (Breaking down the Solar System and Install, will be covered in another chapter) As well as deciding where you are going to want to place your lighting fixtures, switches, electrical outlets, plumbing for your kitchen sink and drain, plumbing for the bathroom sink and drain, the water inlet for the toilet and where the toilet drain is going to be... (Again, the plumbing will also be explained in more detail in another chapter) This is primarily just so you can mark and identify where you want everything located to ensure that you are happy with where everything is going to go before you start drilling holes.

Once you have decided where your utilities are going to go, you are going to want to prevent having any moisture issues on the bottom of your small home. Generally, whenever these structures are built, they will use OSB or similar products on the flooring. These types of materials won't usually stand up well to moisture. If you have an option, I will pay extra to have plywood installed on the flooring and make sure that it is treated to help avoid any issues with moisture later on down the road. The underside of the floor, where it faces the ground, is where moisture will start to form, and bugs can start to eat through. Putting your shed on blocks and getting it up off the ground high enough for you to crawl under and access everything underneath will definitely make things much easier for you to connect all of your utilities, drains, etc, and whenever you need to get under your small home to conduct any kind of ongoing maintenance in the future. It will just make things a lot easier for you in the long run. Even if you don't need to use blocks for leveling your small home on your property, having a way to access the flooring and having a space that will allow airflow under your home will be very important to keep your floor dry from being able to build up any moisture to also help prevent the underside from eventually rotting away. Once you have these

Things accomplished: I would then apply a thick coating of exterior oil-based paint to the underside of your flooring to seal it and help protect the wood against moisture.

Imagine coming home to this Amazing Small Home. With a little imagination an ordinary building can come to life. The possibilities are endless

You will want to do your homework when looking for a good-quality building to convert into your small home. In many cases, builders will use a smaller dimension frame than traditional 2x4's. If you have the option, try to request that your building be built with regular 2x4's so that all of your building materials will work (insulation, electrical boxes, etc, which are all sized for 2x4 cavities) If your walls aren't framed with 2x4's then you may have to figure out other alternatives to every other step during your closing in your walls because all of the building materials are sized to accommodate a 2x4 wall. Not to mention, you are most probably going to want to have a deeper cavity in your walls so you can insulate the walls better for more efficiency. If the walls are framed with 1x3's like is done in most buildings, you will not be able to insulate your home as well because of having thinner wall cavities. However, there is a solution to having deeper wall cavities if your building is built with 1x3 studs instead of using 2x4's then you will just need to try and build your walls inwards, but if you are going to have to go through that kind of trouble, you might want to possibly consider getting a slight building, you might as well just go for thicker walls in order to have more insulation and make your small home more efficient.

Once you have all of this worked out and you have the building you want, it is time to rough in your electrical, water, drains, and HVAC. A Huge Tip I would like to give here before you get started would be to take a video and a lot of photos of the walls and of the areas where you are going to be putting your utilities so you can remember where things are in the future in case you may need to fix something. (a nice little blueprint now could save you a lot of headaches later on).

Start putting in your electrical lines, water lines, drain lines, internet connections, and any HVAC connections that you may need to install. At this time, I would also consider installing electrical outlet boxes and light fixtures on the outside of the building because it will be very difficult to add these in later after everything is all closed up. Take a look around, take your time, consider everything that you will be plugging in, and put an outlet in there. Basically, if you have any electrical runs on your walls of about 5 feet or more with no outlet, just put one there. Outlets and receptacles are pretty cheap, so don't be too cheap to add these in. You will thank yourself later on whenever you need to use one.

Once you have your utilities roughed in and everything looks good, you are going to want to get a few cases of spray foam and silicone caulk and then start sealing everything up. Most of these buildings aren't very airtight, and with that being said, bugs can get in through these air gaps, as well, so start with the space where the roof meets the top of the wall and around the soffit / facia is usually very poorly done and you can usually see daylight there. Follow up by sealing all the junctions, seams, and transition points. 1st start from the outside, then seal again from the inside. Also, seal up where the walls meet the floors, the corners and inside the framing where the studs meet the sheathing. This might seem like it is somewhat excessive, but your building is small and should only take a few hours to get it all sealed up tight; in the end, it will be well worth the extra effort you are putting into it. Look for different areas that you may not be able to insulate easily and go over any that seem to safeguard from having any leaks. You may be saying to yourself that this seems like you are going overboard, but a few hours of your time and about \$50 to \$100 of prevention will pay you back dividends in the future, as well as keeping out any air and water, not to mention it will keep those unwanted bugs from coming in.

I would like to just lightly touch base and add a note about the air quality in your small new home. Since you have taken all this extra effort to seal up your small new home so well, it is time to address the issue by making some kind of provision and thinking about some kind of fresh air exchange as well as having a form of humidity control in your building. Whenever you seal up such a small space that you're going to be living in, you should start thinking about taking your air quality more seriously. My personal suggestion (and favorite) is installing a Mini-Split heating and cooling system (which also dehumidifies the air, as well). Another option would be to install an ERV Unit, otherwise known as an Energy Recovery Ventilation Unit. This will either heat or cool the incoming air through an exchanger and adjust the humidity levels, as well. The ERV Unit will cycle your air so the indoor air quality is always fresh and also produces the correct amount of humidity you will need in your small home. These are just two different options that I would like for you to possibly consider installing one of these systems in your small new home, not only to have safer air quality but also to allow you to have a higher level of comfort in your small new home, as well.

In order to be more comfortable, your home will also need to become more efficient, and you are going to accomplish this by insulating the walls, ceiling, and floors. In your walls and ceiling, you basically have two main options to accomplish this. The two different options are going to be either spray foam or bat insulation. Bat insulation is a good option. It's easy to install and not that expensive. You can get bat insulation that is sized correctly for your wall cavities to minimize the amount of cutting you may need to do. The other option, and the one that I would recommend, is the close-cell spray foam. I would primarily suggest using the closed-cell spray foam because it is also a great vapor and air barrier. Spray foam is also a very high R-Value, so you will be able to keep your small home hot or cold longer with the same amount of wall thickness. Many people will suggest open foam because it's cheaper, or some people will argue that it's easier to find a leak if one occurs. Because your home is a small space, it will be more expensive, but since it's small, you may only be looking at a difference of a few hundred extra dollars. The notion that you can spot leaks easier is something I choose not to believe because it is a new building and all the extra time and preparation you spent making sure everything was sealed tight. I have a hard time accepting that it is going to be leaking anytime soon, and "if" it were to leak, the closed cell foam adheres to the back of the roof decking, reducing the probability of the spread of any leaks. If you were to use the Open Cell Foam, the open cell would allow the water to flow through it and allow water to leak into the wall cavity, which in turn would eventually leave it wet, allowing mold to form.

This will bring us to insulate the floor of your small home. (It's a good thing that you decided to set your small new home up on blocks so that you can crawl under it for this step.) You definitely want to insulate your shed floor, or you'll have a condensing surface that will allow your feet to be cold on the floors.

There are a few ways to accomplish this step, as well. You can use Spray Foam; you could also use Bat Insulation. Although it may be messy, it would work if cost were an issue for you. Since it will be the least pleasurable part of the job because you will have to crawl in and out from under the building, Using Foam Board would be my choice for cleanliness and ease of installation. I prefer to use the 3-inch foam board; it just fills the cavities faster because of its thickness, but you can use whatever size is available for you. Then, measure the spaces between the floor joists and cut your foam board sections to fit. Press the sections until you have filled the cavities, and then close off the bottom with plywood or planks. Then, caulk the seams and paint with waterproof paint to keep out any moisture.

Now, you can move to the inside and begin to make it actually look like a home. Whether you want to install drywall and paint, paneling, tongue and groove planking, or a combination of each, all will definitely bring on the transformation that you've been patiently waiting for. Once you have the walls covered, it is time to trim out your doors and windows and then paint the whole thing inside. Once you've brought the inside to life with color, you can put down your flooring and baseboards to cover any rough edges or gaps along the floor and walls. Put up your lighting fixtures, and whaa-laa ... Now it looks more like a home instead of just a shell. You're Almost there!

Interior Examples: Living Room and Kitchen areas can be as nice as you want it to be

Unless you want custom counters and countertops, consider using some off-the-shelf premade cabinets, countertops, sinks, etc., from the big box store or possibly even Ikea. This will definitely speed things up a lot. Bring in your appliances, and there you go!

YOU DID IT!!! Your Shed to Small Home Conversion is Complete!!

It may seem like it was a lot of work, but look at the time and money you have saved yourself. Think about what this really means for you.

You have moved yourself into a different category of living!!

CONGRATULATIONS!! You're taking the first step to True Freedom.

Where will you go from here?

Small Yard Barns Make Excellent Shed to Home Conversions

CHAPTER 6

WALLS / WINDOWS AND DOORS / INSTALLING THE ROOF / DRYING IN YOUR HOME

I would like to briefly touch base on some of the basic construction aspects you'll need to consider while you are designing and planning out how to build your small home. Depending on what type of structure you are going to choose to build on your property, there are going to be a few different things that you need to be aware of. Whenever you are laying out the design of an earthbag structure, you will need to take into consideration that it has a unique building style. Whenever you are laying out your structure, you will need to decide where you want to put the doors and windows. Once you know where the windows are going to go, you will need to decide what size windows and doors you want to install. After you have decided on the sizes of everything, you will then need to build yourself some forms that you can set on the walls to create the openings for the windows and the doors. Whenever you set the forms down on the row of bags where you want the bottom of the opening to be, you will need to put a few spacers, such as scrap 2x4s or something similar, on each side of the base of the form, creating a gap on the bottom of the form. By putting the spacers under the form, you will be able to remove those spacers from underneath the form, which will allow the form to drop down and give you a small space that's large enough to take the form out of the wall. Something to think about whenever you are building your forms, though, is that the outside dimension of your form will need to be at least 2 inches larger on the sides and on the top than the actual size of the windows that you are planning to install. So, whenever you complete the walls and remove the forms from the structure, this will allow space for leveling and shimming of the windows and doors.

You will also need to remember that as you are building up tour walls in the earthbag structure, you are going to have to put in wooden blocks evenly spaced between some of the rows of bags that will come up flush to the edge of the form opening so that you will have something that you can secure the door frames and window frames to make them solid and secure. Once you have the frames built securely in place and have removed the forms from the openings, you will be able to use your filler mix (same as you are using to fill your sandbags) to mud in around the outside of the door and window frames in order to seal up any openings or voids around the edges to make it airtight and ready for plastering. Spray foam can also be used to fill any gaps around the frame openings to achieve the same results. The same concept would also be used in building a regular Pueblo Style or Casita Style Aircrete Structure using the cast-in-place method. You would just need to make your forms wide enough so that they would be the same thickness as the thickness of the wall forms are going to be, so the forms will slide over the outside of the form as you move upward with each section you are pouring. You would build the forms for your doors and windows in the same way as previously mentioned for the earthbag construction method. Allowing the inside dimensions of your forms to be at least 2 inches larger on the sides and on the top than the actual size of the windows that you are planning to install for leveling and shimming purposes as well. Just remember to make the frames the same width as the thickness of the cast-in-place wall forms. The only difference with these frames is that they are going to stay in the structure as these frames are going to be used to actually secure the door and window frames into place once you are finished with pouring the walls on your home. This is why you are going to make sure that the <u>in</u>side diameter measurements of the doors and window frames are 2 inches larger than the outside of the form. I'd also like to add that whenever you are building the door frames, make sure that you install a second board for thickness on the frame so that it will be more solid and will not flex and fully support the weight of the door. You will also install the pre-hung door jam with the hinges on the side of the frame that has the double board side to it.

If you are building yourself a dome with Aircrete, then the process will be a little different because you will be making your own Aircrete blocks to build your dome structure with. If you are building your dome structure with Aircrete blocks, then you will pretty much use the same construction techniques as you did with the earthbag structure. You will use the same principle for opening the doors by using forms for your framework, as well as the compass arm concept to keep the walls symmetrical and straight as you build your dome structure. You will just be laying blocks as opposed to filling sandbags and wrapping the exterior part of the structure with a fabric cloth or some type of fiber mess cloth to make the surface stronger. Then, once your dome is complete, you can then mark and cut out where you want your window frame to go.

If you are considering doing a shed to home conversion, then this part of the building is pretty much already going to be done for you whenever they build the structure. The main thing you will need to make sure of is that everything is sealed up around the doors and windows. You shouldn't have any issues with anything, and you can speed right past this step because it should already be done for you.

I want to lightly touch base on roofing for each of the three structures. The Earthbag Construction Method, as well as the Aircrete Block Construction Method for building domes, will both pretty much be about the same because the transition from building the walls with the compass will naturally curve or arch up naturally as you continue to build, which at the top of the structure you can then decide whether or not you want to just close up the structure or if you want to add in a skylight of some kind to allow natural lighting to shine into your dome home.

Choosing the straight wall Method or the cast-in-place method for building with Aircrete will require you to add in a concrete and rebar bond beam at the top of your walls so that you will have a stronger surface at the top to secure the rafters or vigas to, depending whether you want to install a pitched style roof or you want to go with a sloped pitch roof for a more authentic looking Pueblo Style building, doesn't matter as long as you put in a concrete bond beam for strength. That roof can then be insulated with foam board or bat insulation to help protect it from intense hot or cold temperatures. You can cover these roofs with rubber liners or metal sheeting; that way, you can still connect in a rainwater collection system to your home.

The only difference with Earthbag Construction for doing a straight wall build is that you may need to add some extra buttressing along your walls to keep them from pushing outward. You would still need to install a cement bond beam as well to be able to secure the particular style roof you want to install on your home, and the insulation and waterproof covering for the roof would also pretty much be the same as described before for the Aircrete Construction and adding in a rainwater catchment system, as well.

Just as before, if you are going to choose the shed-to-home conversion, then this step should already be done for you. The only thing with the shed-to-home conversions is that a lot of the shed manufacturers like to install shingles on their sheds, so you will most likely have to have a metal roof installed whenever you order your building if you are going to be setting up a rainwater catchment system to your small home. Just a word of caution: You <u>DO NOT</u>... Want to do any Rainwater Collection from a roof that has shingles installed? There are toxic chemicals as well as tar in the shingle material, it will make you sick as well as your animals and it's not healthy for any of the plants you may be wanting to grow in the future. I just strongly advise against having a shingled roof unless you do not have any other option for your building when you buy it.

Once you have dried the doors, windows, and roof, the trim is installed around the windows, and everything is sealed up and painted, you can decide what you would like to do for the flooring in your small home. Choosing flooring is also an important step because it needs to add a level of protection, as well as being waterproof and easy to clean. There are several different options you can go with whenever you start installing your flooring; you can go as rustic or as nice as your pockets will allow. If you have built an Earthbag or Aircrete structure and it doesn't yet have a floor, you can add in gravel and sand and compact it down, put down a vapor barrier to hold out moisture, put in some foam board for insulation and install a laminate floating floor over the top for a nice quick floor install. You can do basically the same if you have a cement slab down; you could either add in the vapor barrier over the concrete or then put down your floating laminate flooring. You may want to go all out and get creative with your flooring and install some decorative tile for a very unique and distinctive look. If you're on a budget and just want to get something down, or perhaps you are Looking for a more natural or rustic look, you might consider making an earthen floor. In order to put down an earthen floor, you will need to prepare the area where the floor is going to be. Make sure that it is packed down and leveled so that the additional levels will be of a consistent thickness as you put them down. After Packing and leveling, add a waterproof barrier, such as a sheet of plastic, over the top of the initial surface area you just packed down and leveled out, then put down a thin layer of sand on top. This will hold the plastic in place and keep any water or moisture from wicking up to the surface. Next, you will be making up a cob-style mix that consists of sand, clay and straw: 1 part sand, 1 part clay (depending on the quality of clay) and longer straw pieces. Apply this layer so it is only about 3 ½ inches thick. This thickness will create the base for your floor; once this layer is applied, you must let it dry completely before putting down the next layer. After that layer is dry, then you will prepare a thinner cob-style mix and mix it with chaff- which is chopped straw (short straw pieces), 2 or 3 parts sand, to 1 part clay (depending on the quality of clay) and add in the chaff- which is the chopped straw (short straw pieces). Apply this layer so it is about 1 ½ to 2 inches thick; this will be the center layer for your floor. You must also allow this layer to completely dry before adding the final layer. Once that layer is dry, then you will prepare a mix consisting of 3 parts sand to 1 part clay. Only this time, use finer sand in your mix to allow for a smoother finish on your floor. This layer will only be about 3/8 of an inch to ½ inch maximum. This will become the top layer for your floor and will be the final finish when completed. As you are doing the finished trowel work on the surface, as it is beginning to dry and become firmer, you can spritz a little water on the surface and by using a trowel to blend it in, you will be able to make a really smooth surface on your floor. Again, as stated before, allow this to completely dry, and then you will begin the sealing process. For the sealing process, you are going to use linseed oil and gum trigs or gum trigintine, not to be confused with mineral trigintine, which is a petroleum solvent. Be advised that even though gum turps are a natural product, they still smell very strong, and you will need to have some good airflow/ventilation as well as gloves for skin protection whenever you are working with them. I would apply six different coats to make your floor super hard and give it an amazing finish. Just remember, when you are installing these coats, you must allow each coat to absorb into the surface and dry before applying the next one. This is adding strength to your floor with every coat. You will need to heat/boil the linseed oil to achieve the best results when applying it. Here are the Ratios needed to achieve the desired finish.

1st Coat = 100% Linseed Oil 2nd Coat = 80% Linseed Oil to 20% Turps 3rd Coat = 60% Linseed Oil to 40% Turps 4th Coat = 40% Linseed Oil to 60% Turps 5th Coat = 20 % Linseed Oil to 80% Turps 6th and Final Coat = 100% Turps

I would like to add that although you can just apply Linseed Oil to the surface, it will be fine. Your floor will require regular maintenance and upkeep because it the Linseed Oil by itself will just soak in and not allow the surface to become really hard. I know that this may seem like a lot of work, but remember, it is a very distinct look and offers a totally different option than most people would most likely choose to use. I just thought I would share this option and break it down more for you in case you would like to give it a try. Again, it is an option for a beautiful natural floor.

Alright, now let's move on to the next option. If you happen to have a concrete floor that is fairly smooth, then you could get yourself some concrete stain and do some awesome-looking stained concrete floors. Concrete stain can primarily be done in two ways. It can be applied as an acid stain, which I need to warn you about. It is acid-based, so whenever you use it, it is very toxic, and you should wear a respirator when applying it. It will definitely take your breath away if you are using it indoors; even if you do have it ventilated, it is still very strong if you breathe it into your lungs. Anyway, once you decide on the colors you want, you apply them as per the specified manufacturer's directions and allow them to soak into the surface. Then, you would need to clean and neutralize the acid on the concrete, allow it to dry completely, and apply a sealer to lock in a beautiful look. The issue that I always had with Acid Stains is that acid stains work by having a chemical reaction with the concrete, and by having that chemical reaction, you may not end up with the same color that you thought you were going to be getting as the end result. Although, it will come out looking Great, you may have to just settle with whatever the color comes out to be as the end result because once it's applied, there is no going back and changing it, so you have to be flexible about the colors you may end up with and realizing that you may be stuck with a color you don't want... The other type of concrete stain is an Acrylic Based Stain, which is what I have always preferred to use. It is the opposite of using acid stains. It doesn't have a toxic odor, it will not burn your skin, and whenever you choose your colors, that is pretty much going to be what it looks like whenever you finish with your floor. Whenever I do my Acrylic Based Staining, I like to use color tints, or I will use a good quality silicone-based paint and water it down and add in some acrylic additive before I apply it with either a sprayer, spray bottle, or I will apply it with a sponge. It also dries fairly quickly, so once it's dry, I like to use a natural stone sealer over it to lock in my colors. If I had the option, I like to use a xylene-based sealer as opposed to a water-based sealer just because the xylene-based sealer usually lasts longer than the water-based sealer does. Not to mention that if you are using an acrylic-based stain, it is just more user-friendly to work with. Perhaps you just want to get it covered quickly and be done with it; you can just put down some linoleum or carpeting, put in some baseboards and call it a day. You literally have a ton of options whenever it comes to doing your floors. These suggestions are just a few things you can do to finish out your small home.

There is one more aspect of finishing out your home: giving it that amazing and unique look that could take it to the next level. With that being said, I would like to suggest some exterior wall covering options that perhaps you may have not heard of or even thought about. I was introduced to this product a few years ago, and since I live in the desert, where it gets extremely hot during the summertime, I gave it a try and found it to be a pretty amazing product. So, I would like to share some information about this product with you. The company is called Hy-Tech Thermal Solutions. They offer either premixed or a paint additive that is designed specifically for mixing into paints, coatings, and composites to form a tight interlocking matrix that reduces conductive heat through the painted surface. The ceramic barrier reflects up to 90% of the heat back to the source. One of their statistics is that the microspheres in the HY-TECH insulating ceramic additive have compressive strengths up to 6,000 psi, a softening point of about 1800° C., and they are fairly chemical resistant, with low thermal conductivity of 0.1 W / m / Degrees C. and even though I am not an expert in this specific technical jargon, all I know is that it drastically cuts down on the heat on the outside of your structure, which will keep your home cooler in summer and warmer in the winter. This means it is going to save you money and make your home more comfortable in the long run. I mixed the ceramic additive with an elastomeric-based coating and found that I really liked the results I got. I want to add that I am not affiliated with this company, nor am I compensated by it in any way. I just liked the product, was happy with the results and wanted to share my experience with you and I thought it might possibly be able to help you in some way, as well. If you are interested in trying this product, the website is: http://hytechsales.com/insulating_paint_additives.html

As I said, it could be an option for you. There are several other types of exterior coatings you could also try, such as natural lime plaster, Acrylic based concrete coating, Stucco based covering, Elastomeric Coatings, Metal Cladding, Pre-Cast Stone, Rock and Mortar Coating, Spray Stencil, or Trowel on Cementous Designs. It's really all about where you want to take your creativity if that would be your desire to make your small home truly unique. If your home has straighter walls, such as a shed-to-home conversion, you could do a genuine log cabin look and finish it out with log siding and a realistic stone base for that authentic log cabin appearance that others would be envious of. The sky is the limit when it comes to what your own personal designs and tastes may be.

CHAPTER 7

WATER CATCHMENT SYSTEM / LAYING OUT THE PLUMBING / PERSONAL WATER FILTERS

Installing Waterlines, Water Storage Tanks and Connecting Everything to a Water Pressure Tank so you can have pressurized water in your off-grid home. Build and install your own sewage lines for the septic and the toilet, building your own DIY Septic System with Leach Lines.

In this chapter, I would like to discuss Water Catchment and begin familiarizing you a little with what a rainwater catchment system does, some benefits of having a rainwater catchment system, a few myths about shelf-life, What to look for in Rainwater Collection Storage Containers, Treating the water that is collected in your Storage Tanks, How you can put together your own affordable rainwater catchment system and how to calculate the amount of rainfall into your water tanks. Basically, a rainwater catchment system diverts and stores rainwater, providing a clean, free water source that reduces stormwater runoff as well as demand for potable water supplies. A rainwater catchment system is basically made up of 6 components. 1) The Roof- The roof surface is what catches the rain. 2) Gutters and Pipes- Gutters directly capture the rainwater as it falls from the roof, and the pipes transport the water throughout the system. 3) Leaf Filters- All of the entrances and exits in your system must be covered with a filter of some kind to keep out leaves, trash, and even small animals and insects from being able to get into your system; this filter can be as simple as using a fine mesh screen material or even by cutting up an old T-Shirt and wrapping it around the entry and exit point of your system. 4) First Flush- A first flush system separates the first harvested rain from each rainfall to ensure that the rainwater that enters your main water storage tank is as clean as possible. It will keep dust, leaves, mud, debris, animal droppings and any potential biological organisms from entering your tanks. Water collected in a first flush system is not meant for drinking or cooking but is great for watering your garden. There are different types of first flush systems that can be constructed with barrels or IBC Totes, PVC Piping, Pex Pipe, or other types of containers. 5) Cistern or Large Tank- This is the main storage for your harvested rainwater, and it can either be free-standing or buried underground. 6) Biological Treatment- Rainwater is free of chemicals, heavy metals, and minerals, but it is still at risk for pathogens, bacteria, and other biological contaminants. Always treat your rainwater collection system for these contaminants before consuming them. Just to add as a note* Rainwater Collection, in combination with biological treatment, is a safe, healthy, and sustainable water solution.

3,000 Gallon Water Storage Tank and Tank Shut Off Valve

Some of the benefits of rainwater collection is that rainwater is a relatively clean and free source of water. This means that you have total control over your water own water supply (not like being in a city with water restrictions), it's socially acceptable and environmentally responsible, It promotes self-sufficiency and helps preserve water, It reduces stormwater run-off from your home, It can help save drainage problems on your property while providing you with free water, It uses simple technologies that are inexpensive and are easy to maintain, It can be used as a main source of water or a backup source to your well, your system can be flexible and can be modular in nature-allowing expansion, reconfiguration or relocation if necessary and it can be an excellent source of back-up water during emergencies.

There are a lot of people out there who will tell you that drinking rainwater isn't safe. I believe this to be the case mainly because they are uneducated as to exactly what rainwater collection is all about. However, my biggest question for them would be that if rainwater isn't safe to drink, then how on earth did our grandparents and their grandparents survive from drinking rainwater way back before there were all of these high-priced commercial and highly technical, sophisticated water filtration systems? It's a simple question, actually, yet there are people out there who will want to argue and debate that rainwater harvesting isn't safe for you to drink because most of them only believe what they hear from others or hear from the media. Now, Granted, I understand that people are frightened of germs, parasites, bacteria and so on, and they do have a right to be concerned because there have been people who have gotten sick from "bad water," so to speak. I also agree and want to clarify that before you decide to drink any kind of water, you don't know if the source it came from is clean and pure, that yes, by all means, that water should be tested and verified that it is indeed safe to drink before consuming it. However, I am talking about the

"Rainwater Collection," which is not drinking from rivers, springs, lakes, or natural streams. That is a different topic altogether, with many other variables to consider. This rendering is only meant to be targeted at "rainwater collection" and "storage of rainwater." There is a common myth that water expires; this is simply not true. Water doesn't go bad or expire but can only become biologically or chemically contaminated. If you have had water stored for a long time and it has a stale taste, that is not the water expiring; in fact the taste can be removed merely by rotating and purifying your water. If your water started out clean yet has been stored for some time in a cool, dark, and dry area, and it has not been directly on concrete and has been stored away from harmful chemicals and harsh fumes, or your tanks are buried in the ground with a shade over then to keep them out of sunlight, then water can technically be stored indefinitely. However, you should try to rotate this water from time to time to keep it fresh, as it may give you some peace of mind. There is another myth that it is ok to store water in just about any plastic container you have available. This is definitely not true. If you want to store water for any amount of time, it needs to be stored in metalized bags or UV-Resistant Plastic Containers. It is also worth keeping in mind that Blue is the color of a suitable water storage container. This color limits light exposure, which in turn hinders the growth of algae and bacteria. The safest water storage containers are Poly-Based Plastics, or plastics numbered #1, #2, and #4. Most quality containers in the market are fashioned from plastic #2. This kind of plastic is great for long-term use. If you have any questions about what kind of plastic a container is made of, the number of plastics used to create the container should be marked on the bottom of the container. Avoid using milk jugs for storing water long term, as they are biodegradable and thus will decompose as time passes. Live cultures from the milk that remains in the jug will make you sick if consumed with drinking water that has been stored for a long time. No type of disposable bottles is also a good idea for storage in the long term. You can use soda bottles for long-term storage. However, it is important to keep in mind that plastics absorb flavors, and because of this, water stored might end up having a little bit of a soda taste to it. As such, it might not be suitable for cooking.

Since we touched base a little on water storage containers, now let's take a look at how to treat the rainwater that you are going to collect into your storage tanks. I am going to try to keep this simple. So, for ease of understanding and for the purpose of this book, we are just going to say that you have a 500-gallon water Storage Tank in which you are collecting your rainwater. The recommended amount of Standard Unscented, Non-Detergent Household Chlorine Bleach (5.25% Concentration). You can look for name brands such as Clorox or Purex. For Each 500 Gallons that you are going to treat, you will put in 1 to 1 ½ Fluid Ounces or (2 to 3 Tablespoons) of bleach into your 500-gallon water Storage Tank. This should keep your water clean and safe. So, if you have a larger tank, just add in this amount for every additional 500 Gallons you have. -If you have a 275 Gallon IBC Tote that you are collecting your water in, then you would only put about half of the amount of bleach to treat your IBC Storage Tank with about 1 Fluid Ounce or (2 Tablespoons) in your 275 Gallon IBC Tote. -If you only have a Blue 50 Gallon Plastic Drum, then add about ½ Ounce or 1 Tablespoon of Standard Unscented, Non-Detergent Household Chlorine Bleach

(5.25% Concentration) to your Water Barrel. -If you have a smaller amount of water that you would like to treat: 1 Quart Water / 5 Drops Bleach ½ Gallon Water / 10 Drops Bleach 1 Gallon Water / ¼ teaspoon Bleach 5 Gallons Water / 1 teaspoon Bleach 10 Gallons Water / 2 teaspoons Bleach -If you are curious about boiling rainwater for purity. Most health organizations, including the Center for Disease Control, recommend that you boil water vigorously for 1 minute up to elevations of 2,000 meters (6,562 feet) and 3 minutes at elevations higher than that. You are guaranteed to be safe from giardia and crypto if you follow those guidelines. Without a doubt, all water catchment systems should be purified before being consumed. Using Unscented laundry bleach is one way of doing this. It is an inexpensive way to kill many of the bacteria and algae that may be present in your water storage tank.

Example of a 275 Gallon IBC Tote

This is merely an average of what the majority of people use... as well as what they recommend using in their own rainwater/bleach ratios for their water storage tanks. It's what I use, and I have had very good luck with it. I have used a bit more of the bleach in the water before, but a word of caution: if you put too much bleach in the water, your water will smell like chlorine, and it will end up having a bit of a bleachy taste to it. However, if you accidentally happen to add in a little too much bleach, all you need to do is add in some more water, and that will take care of it. One thing I would advise is that once you add the bleach into your water tank, let it sit for at least an hour before drinking it. But, by all means, experiment and see what you prefer, but don't use any less bleach than what is recommended because you need to have a certain amount of bleach in your water to effectively treat your water system. *A note that I would like to add here is that if you are going to use an IBC Tote for your water storage, make sure that you get yourself some cheap black spray-paint and completely paint your IBC Tote on ALL 4 SIDES and the TOP. No need to buy expensive spray paint. It just needs to be completely dark to keep the light out and to keep any algae from growing inside of it. I know of a few people who have painted their IBC Totes a Desert Tan Color, as well and have not had any trouble with Algae Growth, but I, myself, would just go with the black because I just feel more comfortable with using the black to darken them out.

Now that you are thinking about what type of different container or containers that might be most suitable for your rainwater catchment system, something you must consider at this point is water filtration and purification. Although you are going to be treating your water storage tanks, that may not be enough to weed out other possible contaminants that could affect your water system. I would like to share a few different options that I hope can help bring you some peace of mind and possibly relieve any concern you may be having about filtering and purifying the water from your rainwater collection system. You will find that there are several different options for drinking water purification systems when you start doing your own internet search, which can also be confusing as well as can get very costly if you listen to all of the technical hype and statistics everyone will push on you as to why their systems are the best for you and your family. I will give you my take on a few different systems, their capacities, and basic costs, and then you can form your own opinion on what might be the best fit for you. Now, keep in mind that I am mainly talking about lower cost, simple systems for drinking water that you can use in your small, off-grid home and won't break the bank. The systems I am going to mention can fit a variety of different situations. Whether it is just you... you, and a friend, if you have a family or group of people. I believe that one of these water systems could be the perfect fit for you and your situation. OK, now, with that being said. The first small system that a lot of people will swear by is the Big Berkey Water Filter System. It comes in stainless steel, is very simple to set up, and is a very easy-to-use system with a 2.25 gallon capacity and a lifespan of about 6,000 gallons. You can run through the system before you need to change out the filters. It measures about 21 inches tall and about 8.5 inches wide, so it will sit on your counter or tabletop just fine. This system has received great reviews from thousands of people who have used it over the years. It is a very popular system. The biggest issue for me is the cost of the system. At the time of my writing this book, the Big Berkey Water Filter System is around $400. It comes with two extra filters, and you also have the option to purchase additional chloride filters to add to your system if you choose. To me, that is a lot of money, but it will definitely serve you well and will most likely be able to supply you with clean, filtered drinking water for over a year. For me, an alternative system to this would be to make your own DIY Berkey Style Water Filter System using 2, 5-gallon Food Grade Plastic Buckets. These buckets with lids can be purchased about anywhere and would probably be less than about $10 Bucks' You would need to purchase a separate water spicket to install on the bottom of the bottom bucket, which you could get at about any hardware store and would only cost you a couple of bucks. The largest cost here would be to just go to the Berkey website or Amazon and order 2 of the replacement filters for the Berkey Water Filter System. These would cost you about $150 for two filters. Yes, it is still a lot of money to me, but at around half the cost, you would be getting the same quality of filtered and purified water as you would get from the original Big Berkey Water Filter System, not to mention you would be getting about twice the amount of filtered and purified water storage as you would get from the Big Berkey Water System since you have 5

Gallons of Storage instead of 2.25 Gallons. Just something to consider. This option isn't made of Stainless Steel...but again, at about half the cost, you should consider that this will keep you supplied with Fresh Purified drinking water for the entire year and beats having to continually go buy water bottles, not to mention all of the waste that the bottles create. I have a few more options for you to consider trying out. Another option that I would like to share with you is The Lifesaver Jerry-Can. It has a cost of around $300 and can be purchased on Amazon. It has a 5-gallon capacity and filters about 20,000 liters of water, which is the equivalent of about 5,300 gallons of drinking water. It can be set on your counter, tabletop or even be taken along in the back of your vehicle for an outdoor excursion. Lastly, I would like to mention the LifeStraw Community – High Capacity, long-lasting Water Purifier. It costs around $350, and it can be purchased on Amazon as well. It holds 50 liters or 13 gallons and will purify about 26,000 gallons of clean drinking water. It's advanced purification technology removes (Rotavirus, Hepatitis A), protects against bacteria (including E. coli, Salmonella), parasites (including Giardia and Cryptosporidium), microplastics, organic chemical matter and also protects against dirt, silt, and sand. These are a few of the water filter systems out there that I think would be a good fit for an off-grid type of environment. These systems have been proven in many different countries and in many different harsh environments known to have problems with contamination in their water. I would also like to add that I AM NOT affiliated with any of these companies in any way, nor do I receive any kind of compensation for any of these products and in my own personal opinion, feel that these products could be a good fit for anyone living off-grid that may have any concerns about purifying their drinking water and as such, these filtration systems do not require any type of electricity or special provisions to operate. Water Filtration is a subject that I could go on and on about and will most likely be elaborating more on actually setting up my own cheap and practical 300 liters per day system in some upcoming information and potential course content that would greatly benefit everyone, but I think I have covered more than enough on this topic for now.

You are going to have to decide where you want to place your storage tank/container. Whether it will be installed closer to the house or away from the house, you will need to determine where you want it to be. You will need to orient the tank so that it can supply the water to your home. You are going to have to run a main water line from the tank to the home once you get ready to hook everything up. However, you are also going to have to decide where the best place might be for you to put all of your (pump utilities). Such as the water pump and tank, the pressure regulator, the one-way check valve, the pressure air tank, tank manifold, etc (I will be explaining this more in a bit, to clarify everything better.) Since I have covered a little about water collection, water storage and with water filtration and purification, I would like to do a brief walkthrough about how you would connect your water catchment system to your new small off-grid home. *Note... As I had stated before, to make a rainwater catchment system, you need to have a metal roof in order to collect the rainwater you will need in order for it to be healthy for consumption. Just to reiterate, You CANNOT use a Shingled Roof for rainwater collection because the petroleum products and chemicals in the shingle material will make you sick. You start off with your rainwater collection system being the roof of your home. Adding any other square footage from other buildings or structures would definitely be a huge benefit because having a larger area for the rainwater to collect on would definitely fill your storage tanks much faster each time it happens to rain. Focusing on the square footage of your roof area is definitely most important, and next, you will need to add gutters around the base of your roofed structures as a place for the rainwater to run off of. You will then need to install some more guttering, or you will need to install piping into your gutters. Once the rainwater has run off the roof structures and into the gutters, the rain will need to be carried to your holding tanks in order to build up your water reserves. Before you actually connect your piping to the storage tanks, you will need to add a screen or some type of filter element so it can catch any of the contaminants that may be washed off the roof once it starts raining. Also, you will want to make sure that the opening where the piping goes into the storage tank is totally sealed off so that small animals, insects, or other debris will not be able to get into your water reserves. This will get the water from your rooftop into your storage tanks. Your storage tank will need to have an overflow port as well as a discharge port installed in order for it to work effectively. The overflow port will need to be installed towards the top of the tank. This way, once the tank is full, it can then either flow over into another tank to continue to increase your water storage capacity, or it will need to be diverted out of the tank once it is full and away from the water tank area to prevent the ground from becoming flooded and making a huge potential mess around your tank. If you have to divert your overflow water from your storage tank, then you may want to possibly consider putting in a small pool or pond close by for an additional water storage reserve if you are not able to install additional tanks. Next, you will want to have a discharge port at the bottom of your storage tank. This will be the outlet that will be plumbed into your home so you can have run water. When the discharge port comes out of the water storage tank, make sure you install a shut-off valve at this location in case you may have to conduct some maintenance on your water system sometime. Doing this will save you a lot of trouble later on down the road when you need to perform some maintenance on your system. After the shut-off valve comes out of your water tank, you will then want to install a water line to where you are going to have your (what I like to call) pump utilities.

*Note. I also like to use Pex-Tubing and Pex-Fittings. I mainly use them because of the ease of maintenance in case of a leak or if I want to move something later on. I prefer Pex-Tubing over PVC because Pex-Tubing not only seems to last a little longer but is also a lot faster to install. PVC tends to break down over time, and the joints can also become weaker. However, Pex-Tubing is a little more expensive than regular PVC, but I feel that it is definitely worth the additional cost as well as the time it will save you when you're doing an install.

Once you have decided on the location of where you want your tank and where you want your tank utilities to be, it is time to connect your water line to the tank and connect the other end of that waterline to where your tank utilities are going to go. I installed all of my tank utilities inside a small box that I built so that I could close everything up during the wintertime to keep everything from freezing up. The pipe on the right side in the left picture is the inlet coming from the storage tank.

As you can see from the picture above, it is a simple box constructed of ripped 2X4s and cheap plywood. Depending on your environment, you may just need to install an enclosure over the front, or you could insulate the sides and front with foam board, install a heat lamp that you can plug in on really cold days/nights, etc.

The One-Way Check Valve is installed on the waterline coming up in front of the tank and going into the inlet of the water pump. This keeps the water pump primed so you can maintain water pressure.

From the top (outlet) of the water pump, the water line is then connected to the manifold of the Pressure Tank. A Water Spicket is also installed onto the manifold so you can open the line from the pump for system bleeding or flushing out and to be able to get unwanted air out of the system or to help prime the pump. The additional outlet on the manifold is for a pressure gauge but isn't installed on this system because the water pump assembly already has a gauge installed to monitor water pressure in the system. An additional shut-off valve is installed on the outlet end of the manifold in case you need to shut off the water going into the house in order to perform any maintenance on the system. The waterline on the left is the outlet line, and this is the one that you will connect to the home's inlet. This is, of course, is a basic layout of how your water collection system can be connected to your home, but it should explain the layout well enough that you should now be more familiar with how this system is going to work. Setting up your rainwater collection system in this manner is simple and fairly inexpensive. It can easily be done on a budget as you have access to the materials. The small shallow well pump came from Harbor Freight and was very reasonable in price. It has everything you need to hook up your water in order to have pressure in your water system. It has a built-in air tank for pressure and a built-in regulator, so it comes on and goes off when pressure is built up. It is a very practical yet easy way to get water to your home. The only thing that you really need is the one-way check valve prior to the waterline going into the pump so your pump will not lose its prime. This system could also be installed without using the additional blue air tank, but the additional air tank allows you to keep consistent water pressure without the pump having to run as much. Therefore saving power or having to run a generator. This pump can also be used with a mid-sized generator if you are not connected to the grid. I have used it many times with my small 5K Generator. A nice asset to have when you need to run water, not to mention being able to take a real shower when you need to.

CHAPTER 8

BUILDING YOUR OWN DIY SEPTIC SYSTEM WITH LEACH LINES

In the last chapter, I went over how to set up a rainwater collection system along with some of the benefits, such as treating your storage tanks, drinking water filtration and purification, and how to hook it all up to your home. In this chapter, I would like to discuss your wastewater, sewage, and a few different types of septic systems, as well as the different ways you can build a DIY septic system with leach lines for your off-grid small home.

The first and most basic system you can use to address the issue of what to do with your solid waste would be a composting toilet. A composting toilet can be a very simple setup to use that basically requires nothing more than using a bucket and sawdust to cover the waste and then dumping it out into a composting bin whenever the bucket gets full. There are, however, several companies out there that specialize in different kinds of composting toilet systems. The biggest benefit of my book is that it doesn't require any water to flush like a regular toilet, and if maintained properly, they do not leave a nasty smell behind. So, basically, it just kind of comes down to a choice of what you prefer to deal with whenever it comes to messing with a compost toilet. In general, most septic systems are made up of two parts: the holding and digesting tanks and the dispersal field, also known as the leach line. As the first holding tank fills up, the liquid waste will transfer to the second tank. Once the second tank fills with liquid, it will disperse into the soil below it. I would like to share a small system with you that is pretty much designed for limited use by two people with no laundry. Now, the tank is much smaller than is required by building codes, and the design is missing some important items, such as internal baffles and getting a qualified site assessment by a septic company. This system uses two Plastic 55 Gallon Barrels, as opposed to the 1,000 to 2,000 Gallon Tanks that are used for a standard conventional home septic system. This system also has a dispersal field/leach line of about one-third that of a large home would have. I just want to add a disclaimer here that anyone planning to build a system similar to this one should be aware that this system most likely would not pass inspection from any public health department and could possibly subject the property owner to a fine if the system was discovered and in use. However, I believe that it is better to dispose of your waste safely than not properly. By using today's water-saving toilets that use less than two gallons per flush, this system will more than adequately handle such a load, and for people living in places without any septic treatment, I believe that it could also be a lifesaver for them. So, just use your best judgment with whatever you decide to do. Since this book is mainly about insights into off-grid building, I am only going to go through the steps required how to build this simple DIY, Plastic 2-Barrel Septic System. However, in the future, I am planning on adding this subject content along with some of the other off-grid course creation material that I am in the process of developing, which I know will help teach you and others exactly how this is done. So, with that being said, let me get started explaining how you can build Your Own Simple DIY, Plastic 2-Barrel Septic System.

Step 1) You are going to cut a hole in the top of each drum that's the same size as the toilet flanges outside measurement. Measure the outside diameter of the toilet flange you're using. Place the hole against the edge of the drum so you can easily connect them

to the pipes. Use a saws-all or hole saw to cut through the barrels. Step 2) Attach a 4-inch toilet flange to each hole. Push the flanges into the top of each tank so they fit flush. Screw the flanges into the tanks so they don't move or shift after you put them in place. Step 3) Cut a 4-inch hole in the first barrel on the opposite side as the hole in the top. Place the hole about 4 to 5 inches down from the top of the barrel and make sure it lines up with the hole on top of the tank. Cut the hole out using a saws-all or a hole saw. Step 4) Next, cut two holes in the side of the barrel at 45-degree angles from the center of the hole on top. Find the center line running through the middle of the hole on top of the barrel. Make 45-degree angles from either side of the centerline and mark it on the second barrel. Use a saws-all or hole saw to cut through the side of the barrel and make your holes. You are now going to be placing your tanks underground. Step 5) You are now going to dig a trench that's 4 feet × 26 feet × 3 feet.

You will need to dig this out with a shovel, backhoe, or an excavator to prepare the spot where you want your DIY Septic Tank to be. Dig out your area until the hole is 4 feet wide, 26 feet long, and 3 feet deep. Step 6) Place the barrel with one side hole at the end of the trench. Make sure the drum is level when you set it down. Check that the top of the barrel is at least 4 inches below the surface before continuing. Step 7) Now, dig a hole in front of it 1 ft deeper for the placement of the second barrel. Make your hole the same diameter as the barrel you're placing in it so it has a tight fit so it will not move around. Step 8) Make sure you level the hole with gravel until the 90-degree fitting fits from the hole in the side of the top barrel to the toilet flange of the lower barrel. At this time, you will only want to dry-fit the 90-degree fitting between the 2 barrels to see if the holes line up evenly. Dig the hole slightly deeper if you need to line the pipeline and flange line up better. Step 9) Cut 3 $\frac{1}{2}$ inch and 2 $\frac{1}{2}$ inch pieces of 4-inch ABS pipe and glue them onto the fitting. Now, you are going to cut the ABS pipe pieces, or nipples, with a hacksaw. Then, the pieces are fitted into the fitting, and PVC glue is used to secure them. Step 10) Test the fit of the pieces for proper alignment between the two barrels. Fit the end of the 2 $\frac{1}{2}$ inch nipple into the side hole on the first barrel. Make sure the nipple on the other end lines up with the hole on top of the second barrel. Step 11) Now glue the end of the 3 $\frac{1}{2}$ nipple into the toilet flange on the second tank. Use PVC glue to secure the fitting. Don't worry about the connection to the first barrel yet since you are going to be connecting it later. Step 12) Glue a Y-fitting to a 3 $\frac{1}{2}$ inch nipple and add a 45-degree fitting to the angled portion of it. Use your PVC glue to secure a nipple to the end of the Y-fitting. Next, align the angled pipe on the Y-fitting so it meets the incoming waste line, and glue it onto the toilet flange. Step 13) Cut and glue the 2 $\frac{1}{2}$ inch nipples to one end of the 45-degree fittings and insert them in the side of the lower barrel, and point the ends of the 45-degree fittings so they are perpendicular to the bottom of the trench. Now You are Going to Connect the Drainpipes Step 14) Now you are going to pound a stake into the ground so that the

top of the stake is level with the bottoms of the 45-degree fittings. It doesn't matter what kind of stakes you use. Just drive the stakes into the ground using a mallet or a hammer. Step 15) Now, tape a 1-inch-wide block to the end of a 4 ft level to help make sure that you create a slope for the drainpipes so that your tanks will empty out. Step 16) Place another stake about 3 $^{1/2}$ feet down the trench from where you put the first one. Now, use your hammer or mallet to drive the stake down until it's the same height as the first one. Step 17) Lay the end of the level without the block on the first stake and the block on the second. Pound the second stake down until the level is balanced. The second stake is now 1 inch lower than the first, or $\frac{1}{4}$ inch lower per 1 foot. Step 18) Repeat this process until you have staked the entire length of the trench. Just continue adding stakes down the rest of the trench every 3 $^{1/2}$ feet from the last one so the stakes will slope away from the plastic barrels. Step 19) Place gravel in the trench until the top of the gravel is level with the top of the stakes. The gravel will now slope away from the barrels at $\frac{1}{4}$ inch per 1 foot of horizontal distance. Step 20) Place 20 feet of perforated drainpipe onto each hole on the second barrel

and slide the ends of the drainpipes into the 45-degree fittings on the lower barrel. Make sure the holes in the pipes face down so liquids can soak back into the ground. Step 21) Now check the pipes with the level to see if the $\frac{1}{4}$ inch grade is consistent along the entire length of the pipe. Adjust the slope by adding or removing gravel under the pipe as required. Step 22) Seal the 45-degree fittings and the 90-degree fittings to the lower and upper barrels, and use either a 2-part epoxy or silicone caulk in order to get the best seal you can on your drainpipes. You could also try using a flex pipe for this so that if the ground shifts, it will also give a little. Step 23) Fill the lower barrel with water to prevent it from collapsing under the weight of the gravel. Bury the trench to the top of the bottom barrel with the remaining gravel. Step 24) Lay landscape fabric over the top of the gravel. This will prevent the soil from seeping into the gravel and ensure that you will have good drainage on your tanks. Step 25) Fill the remaining trench area with soil, compacting it to the original grade. Make sure the ground is level when you finish filling the area with your soil. Leave the top pipe from the first tank exposed so you can easily access the tanks if you need to drain them out later on. Step 26) Now, fill the upper barrel with water. Pour the water directly down the exposed pipes from the top barrel and continue filling the barrel until it's full and place a cap on top of the fitting to seal it after it is full.

This was a pretty in-depth instruction on how to build your own 2-Barrel DIY Septic System. I just wanted to walk you through the process so you would be able to see what is involved in actually installing this Septic System. Another DIY septic system that a lot of people build that is very similar is that they basically build the same exact system, except they use IBC Totes to construct their system instead of using plastic 55-gallon barrels. All of the principles are almost exactly the same, except that it is a much larger system because of the difference in size of the IBC Totes, and although it may seem like a lot of work to install, it is still considerably cheaper than having to hire a company to install one for you, however, as a reminder. This system would not likely pass any kind of state or city inspection, but it is a way to address the issue of your solid waste if you don't have any other option.

Although the above system is small, it still has the same basic properties that are prevalent in the average septic system that almost everyone in the world is familiar with today. I would like to introduce a fairly new method of sewage treatment that you may or may not have heard of. This method of sewage treatment is called "Vermicomposting" The simple definition of vermicomposting is the use of earthworms to convert organic waste into fertilizer. It is basically as simple as that. Vermicomposting flush toilets in particular, is what I would like to share with you. It is the on-site processing of domestic sewage with worms. Vermicomposting sewage systems isn't anything new by any means, but I would like to share with you how some of the basic open-source principles with non-proprietary technology and low-cost components can work, and many of these things can be sourced from existing waste streams. Vermicomposting toilets are an alternative to latrine-style microbial composting toilets. They prove far superior in mass reduction, pathogen destruction, and compost quality at a much lower operational cost than operating conventional toilets. The beauty of this system is in its straightforward simplicity, which it achieves without compromising the ecological principles that govern its function. It needs no external energy input or machinery. It's proved itself over 20 years of trouble-free use where more complex and expensive proprietary technology has sometimes failed. Unlike most other low-tech DIY methods of composting human waste, it allows for the use of conventional flush toilets. This removes the principal objection many people have to composting toilets. Potentially, it could encourage greater decentralization of sewage processing, taking pressure off overloaded municipal facilities and transforming human waste from an environmental pollutant into a valuable resource. Technologically, it's no more complex and much more efficient than a traditional septic tank system and, where local regulations permit, can easily be installed and maintained by any competent DIYer. Maintenance and use require less effort than many dry composting methods, and the system is odor-free. So, when it comes to a Vermicomposting system, what is the maximum number of people that it can handle? That's a Good Question. Given optimum conditions, adult worms can double their numbers in as little as one month and certainly within two months, so the population can quickly adjust to ideal levels and become self-regulating thereafter. Once established, the system can then cope with larger numbers of users over the short term with ease and doesn't need any intervention to do so. With a density of 3kg worms, the maximum density found consistent with a healthy ecosystem would theoretically be capable of handling the regular input of about 12 people. However, based on the information I have been able to find during my own research at the time of writing this book. The estimated maximum usage number of a single IBC-based vermicomposting system has yet to be determined because the average usage studies haven't yet been tested. So, based on the size of the single IBC-based system calculated off of the usage of a larger system average. I would recommend that this size of system be used with no more than four people on a consistent basis.

The following images give a basic description of the material makeup and build layout of a Vermicomposting Toilet System Using a Single-Based IBC Tote.

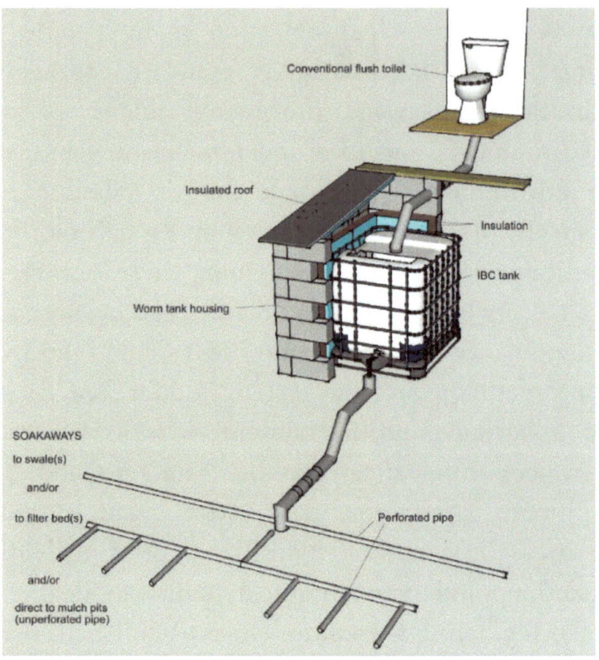

<u>Forward View:</u>

Basic Build Layout of a Vermicomposting Toilet System Using a Single-Based IBC Tote

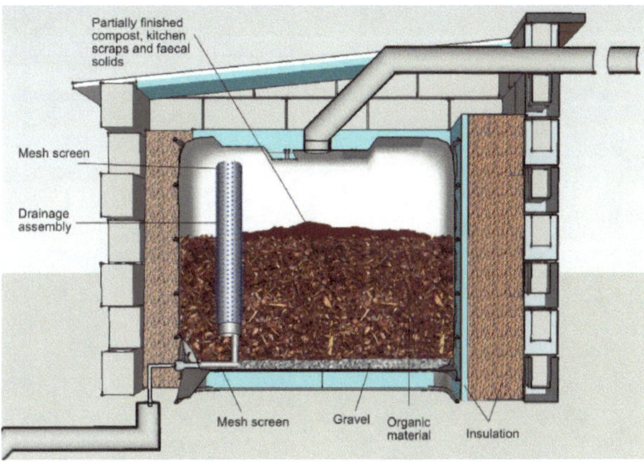

<u>Side View:</u> Basic Build Layout of a Vermicomposting Toilet System Using a Single-Based IBC Tote

Running the Piping: Step 1) Run the pipework to the tank in the standard size for what your toilet is, and make sure that you adhere to the minimum drain slope guidelines for the diameter of pipe that you're using over the horizontal runs to prevent clogging of any solids getting left behind. However, the final drop going into the tank can exceed these slopes. Make sure that you plumb the pipework through the central access hole at the top center of the IBC tank. This is important because it ensures even distribution of waste and helps the worms stay better insulated from external temperature fluctuations if they're encouraged to congregate in the center of the tank.

Tank Drainage: Step 2) When getting ready to install the drainage system in your tank, you will want to get a large diameter pipe and drill several holes in the drainpipe so that it will be able to drain easily. You can see the excessive number of holes in the image below.

<u>Example:</u>

Drainpipe that is installed on the inside of the Single-Based IBC Tote. *Note: Number of holes that will need to be drilled for proper drainage.

Step 3) Once you have drilled all of the holes into the drainpipe, find the different-sized fittings to reduce the pipe to the size of the outlet valve that is on the exit tap housing on the bottom of the IBC Tote. A watertight fitting is not necessary – drainage potential for the tank needs to be maximized. Once you install the perforated drainpipe, the assembly will be held vertically by Gravel at the bottom of the tank. *Note: Make sure that the elbow fitting at the bottom that is connected to the exit tap housing has a hole drilled in the bend, as shown in the picture. It will help drainage at this level because it will be submerged in the gravel and will not need to be wrapped in screen or mesh material.

Step 4) Once the pipe assembly is in place, wrap the pipe with a screen or nylon mess. This will keep the holes from being clogged and will keep debris out of the drainpipe so it can drain through roughly. Step 5) Add another layer of screen or mesh on top of the gravel to prevent the fine worm compost from leaving the tank. This will also keep the organic matter and the worms from passing through the system. Don't use metal – it will rust.

Step 5) Once the assembly is in place, the tank can be filled with organic matter. It is now time to start the Eco-System: Fill the tank 3/4 full of coarse organic material. Use a good mix of woody materials and make sure they're well mixed up. The aim is to have a range of materials that decompose very slowly right through to reasonably fast. This ensures a steady supply of carbon for the ecosystem and provides a relatively stable matrix for the microorganisms to inhabit. Coarse wood shavings and offcuts, chopped pruning, dead leaves, dead bracken, and straw, both dry and partly decomposed. This will make an ideal mix. Keep green material to an absolute minimum. You don't want to encourage too much thermophilic decomposition because the environment will become too hot for the worms. *Note: Fine materials like sawdust should *not* be used. It's too fine and will clog the filters. The materials need to be well mixed up. As mentioned before, dead leaves can stick together when they're wet and form a mat that can cause difficulty in the tank draining properly. If the organic material is very dry, it will benefit from an initial thorough wetting to provide the optimal moisture level for the worms. Hose down the material evenly until water runs from the tank. This also acts as a test to make sure water is draining through properly and fast enough to keep conditions in the tank nicely aerobic.

Once the organic material has been added, cover the surface with a small layer of any or all partially finished compost, animal manure and kitchen scraps. The tank is now ready for worms. Partially finished compost is particularly good as it will contain many of the organisms your ecosystem will need. Worms can be sourced from any animal manure pile where they naturally congregate. (They may not be present in winter, though or during droughts or periods of heavy rainfall.) They can be acquired by mail order in many countries. The preferred species is Eisenia Foetida, also known as the redworm, brandling worm, panfish worm, trout worm, tiger worm, red wiggler worm, or red Californian earthworm. The initial number of worms you'll need depends on how many people will be using the system. A 2011 study conducted in India by Yadav et al (*) found that the optimal stocking density of worms for the fastest reproduction and growth rate was 0.5kg worms/m^2 (1lb per square yard). Since the tank is 1m^2 in cross-sectional area, you can, therefore, start the vermicomposting toilet system with as little as 0.5kg worms. Yadav also found that for optimal food intake by worms, a feedstock rate between 0.40-0.45kg (roughly 1lb) feed per 1kg worms per day was best. On average, humans eliminate 128g (4-5oz) of fresh feces per person per day, so you can calculate the initial number of worms you'll need by allowing 0.5kg (1lb) for every two people using the system. These numbers should keep odors to a minimum while the ecosystem establishes and the worm population grows and adjusts to the feed rate. It's not necessary to be too exacting about this. It's a self-regulating ecosystem. In other words, the worms will adjust their population automatically to move in step with the availability of food. If you're able to allow the worms to adjust to their new environment for a month or so before using the system for the first time, you will minimize the likelihood of any slight smells during the settling-in period. Adding a layer of animal manure and kitchen scraps on the surface of the organic material will ensure the worms have plenty of food for this period.

That is a quick rundown of three different types of solid waste systems. They all have different benefits. My favorite system is the Vermicomposting System, hands down. I love the idea of having a flush toilet without having to worry about having a large septic system. The Vermicomposting Toilet System is gaining interest in many parts of the world and has been proven to be an overall better system over and over. However, in the United States, The Conventional Septic tank is still the popular choice by our government mainly because it is still a way that they can force you to be tied to their system of having to pay for services. Unfortunately, if you want to use any of these alternate systems, you are pretty much going to be on your own for the most part. If you're in a location where you can get away with having an alternative style of living, then by all means, this would be the way for you to go. I personally find these different ways totally fascinating. Mainly because these methods do indeed work. You just have to take the chance and do what you need to do regardless of what anyone may say. It's your life, and you need to live it in anyway you can. I used to spend a lot of time wondering what everyone thought of me, and it kept me in a shell. Once I found out about different styles of alternative building and alternative living, it was time for me to start moving forward and stop looking back. The same goes for you. You have to find happiness for yourself and discover what you are meant to do within your own journey, and you shouldn't look back. Live life with a purpose... I know that The Best is Yet to Come for you!!

CHAPTER 9

ELECTRICAL SYSTEM: UNDERSTANDING
CONVENTIONAL SOLAR PROGRAMS / SIZING
YOUR SOLAR SYSTEM / PORTABLE SOLAR
GENERATORS

In this chapter, I would like to briefly discuss some options for electricity for your small off-grid home. When it comes to providing electricity for your home, you can have your electricity connected to the grid, where you will have to pay a connection fee as well as a monthly bill for the amount of electricity that you use month to month. You can greatly reduce your monthly bills by limiting your usage throughout the month, buying more efficient appliances, and finding other ways to heat and cool your home. These are very viable things to do, and people do these things every day to try and cut down on their monthly utility bills. Another option is to use solar power in your small, off-grid home. Since your home is going to have a smaller footprint than the average-sized home most people live in today, connecting a Solar System to your home could definitely be the way to go if you are truly ready to remove yourself from the grid and if you truly want to stop paying those monthly electric bills. Now, there are new programs in some places that will try to sell you on going solar... and will try to offer you different kinds of incentives for joining in on their solar programs. I am here to tell you that in these programs, you are connecting solar panels to your home.

You are not actually going to be able to cash in on the benefits of "going solar" as they would like you to believe because these programs are considered "Grid-Tied" programs. People can believe what they want, but when is "going solar" going to cost you just as much, if not more, than what your monthly electric bill would normally be? Oh, and yes, they would like you to believe that you can finance these programs, and in "X" number of years, it will be paid off, and you will no longer have to pay a power bill. Ok, my first question is, what if you move? That stays with the house you've been paying on. You will then have to start paying the power bill again once you move to your new home. Also, most of these programs that they are selling you on is just helping them put the power back into their power grid because you are "Grid-Tied," and you are not going to be receiving any extra monthly checks to make any kind of a considerable difference like they would like for you to believe. The biggest thing that I think bothered me the most, and what these companies won't tell you until after the fact, is that whenever the power goes out in your area, you are going to also be without any power as well... Yes, that is correct. You are going to be without power, as well, because you are still going to be connected to their power grid, and your system is NOT independent from the power grid, so when the power goes out in your area, you are without power, as well, again because you are going to be "Grid-Tied."

The only thing your "solar system" is doing is giving power back to the power companies, not to help you when the power goes out. They will not tell you any of this until after the fact, and you are enrolled in their programs. I know several people who have done this because they thought they were still going to have power if the power ever went out in their area. In most cases, this is simply not true. So, if you may be or may have been considering doing this, I would have to advise you to do some further research other than what they are telling you. But, if you are totally ok with paying them a monthly bill for something that you can't even use whenever you are going to need it most, then I have to tell you to have at it, my friend. Again, these are just my own Thoughts on their programs. Solar Electric has been a topic of discussion in some form or other for many years. I have a friend who recently shared some things that he had experienced in the recent past. He started using solar back in the 70s, so he has been involved in working with solar for quite some time now. He told me about a scheme that he attempted around ten years ago where he tried to get a large system hooked up at his place for almost free. He told me that he had agreed to a grid-tie in system and qualified for a lot of subsidy money by doing it. He said that he did all the work himself, and his plan was to get all the stuff paid for and then go off-grid completely. He built a barn with the correct angle so that the solar panels would have the best output. The solar array was about 400 feet from his cabin and had a long wire run underground that was 240 volts. He had nearly 6000 watts of solar power, twin inverters for 120 and 240 volts, and a very pricey battery bank with some of the most expensive batteries that were made. He said that in the end, he called it a mistake and a big waste of money and that, yes, it did work, but having to use Incentive money forced him to buy only certain types of equipment that were all way overpriced and that he would never do anything like this ever again. He said that the system still works and has only had a few electronic failures. He told me that the total cost on paper was over $50,000 and that he paid around $16,000 out of pocket, and that it was still not worth it in the end because of the way they had his hands tied in order to do the installation their way. He went on to tell me further that he had done two other installations that were totally off-grid, in the UP. He said that he had used some of the cheapest materials that he could get and could not have been happier with the results he had gotten. He said he had used Wal-Mart Deep-Cycle Batteries at about $79.00 each, and He used Chinese Charge

Controllers at around $15.00 each. A Harbor Freight 3500-Watt Electric Start Inverter Generator for about $640.00, he had bought himself a new $99.00 Chest Freezer and tweaked the thermostat to make it work as a highly efficient refrigerator. He said that the one thing that he was not happy about getting cheap, though, was the inverter. He said that the cheap inverters with the modified sinewave don't make too much of AC Power that was needed and buying cheap for some things but not for others. He then bought a Xantrex 2000 Watt Sine-Wave inverter that he bought for about $360.00 that he had compared to the Outback 2000-Watt Inverter that he was forced to use two of when he did his Grid-Tie Installation that cost Around $2,000.00 each. He said that you could also buy a 2000 Watt Modified-Wave DC to AC Inverter for about $100.00 and that it would work alright, but for some things, it would do as good of a job as what it should have. He said that he found the Xantrex Pro-Watt 2000 Inverter to be a great buy and that the power generation from it was near perfect. He explained to me about Charge Controllers, and he explained that Charge Controllers do 2 Things... 1) They take high voltage from solar panels and lower it to charge the batteries. 2) They isolate the batteries from the solar panels so the panels cannot discharge the batteries when the sun is not out. He said that in an off-grid system that usually has a 12 12-volt battery bank charged by a solar array that is wired 12 to 24 volts and uses a high-end controller, the solar panels can be wired at over 100 volts. He said there is no need to do that on a cabin, though if they are fairly close to the battery bank, many high-end systems will use just one or two charge controllers that might be rated at about 60 Amps each, and if one fails you will lose most of the system, and they are expensive to replace. Now, he uses cheap controllers and often will just use one controller for two panels; that way, if one fails, just a small part of the system is lost, and it only costs around $15.00 to replace, and there was no right or wrongdoing; it this way, he was just sharing some different ways that he has done it. He said he had a background working as an electrician, so he knows the wire basics and that being used to working with AC systems, there was a small learning curve when doing DC Systems. He said that you could basically install a good working system at an off-grid cabin for a couple of thousand dollars and that only you can decide if having the generator running all the time is worth it, but he prefers the silence and not having to worry about watching the generator and having to fill it up in the middle of the night. He said that they also had put up a small electric fence around their sweet corn field that is powered by solar, and it has a solar fence charger and a battery, which has kept the deer and other animals out for many years. I am very glad that I got to speak to my friend John and get a little clarity from his perspective, as well as hear about some of the unique experiences that he has had over the years working with solar. After talking to John, I'd have to say that he pretty much brought out a great point that just because the components in a system are expensive, it doesn't mean that they are necessarily going to be the best ones for your particular solar system. The same goes for your new small off-grid home, and that's why you definitely need to do some homework and figure out what it is you want to do at your cabin and then decide on which system will be the one that's going to fill those needs the best. Which I believe will probably save you a lot of money down the road. I am by no means an expert at building Solar Systems, and I do not make any claims to be, but I do know enough to know when something is way overpriced whenever I'm looking to purchase something. However, I do know enough to know that the solar system I am looking to buy should at least be sized adequately for what I am going to be using it for. I know that two things I need to look for are that 1) I need to make sure that I have enough solar panels to meet what I need, and 2) I need to make sure that I have enough battery storage to store the power I am going to need. These are basic needs, first and foremost. I need to know what exactly I am going to be using in my home so I can calculate how many watts I will be using per day. So, I will need to make a list of all the essential things I will need power for, such as the water pump and how many watts does it use? How many lights am I going to have on in the home? How long will they be used, and how many watts are there for each? Am I going to be using an electric cooktop? If so, then how many watts and how long I will need each day or maybe I will just use propane instead of the electric cooktop so I can save on those watts I will need to use. Perhaps a small freezer that may have a usage rating of around 683 watts per day, or a mini fridge of 635 watts per day, maybe a regular-sized fridge, and so on; how many watts for each and how long do I plan to use these things per day. Next, maybe I want to install a 9000 BTU Mini-Split A/C Heating unit in order to stay cool and comfortable in the summertime. This unit would use about 900 watts, and if I use it for 10 hours a day, then that would be around 9,000 watts for that day. These are definitely some of the things I need to know in order to correctly size the solar system I want to install into my small home so I can have electricity and be as comfortable as I would be in a regular house connected to the grid. Except, if I size my system correctly, I could install the exact sized system I would need, yes of course, there would be an initial cost to purchase and set it all up, but once that cost has been absorbed, I will no longer have to worry about paying any more electric bills. Now, I don't know about you, but for me, that would be a totally amazing feeling. I may not be able to figure in all of the variables in order to get the sizing absolutely correct, but my thought is that if I estimated as best I could, and then added an extra 1000-watt-hours on top of my estimate for incidentals, I may not have known to take into consideration at the time, then I'm pretty dam sure that system would be pretty close to what I would actually need, as opposed to just guessing off the top of my head or possibly spending the money and buying something that I just thought that looked like a good package, might work, then coming to find out I could have probably put together the system I really needed for what the system I bought that wasn't a good fit for what I needed and was left coming up short on the power I needed because the one I bought won't power my A/C system and it's 100 Degrees outside. If that makes sense. All I am saying is that doing a little research on this subject could save you a lot of money later on down the road. Now, I am not saying that there are really good, affordable solar packages out there. I'm just saying that you should know what kind of system you are going to need before possibly purchasing something that may not be right for you. If you are really serious about wanting to know how to build your own complete solar system that will power a small off-grid home with most of the things I listed in the example above, I will be building and installing this exact system in my own small off-grid home. I will soon be releasing a separate course that will show you exactly how you can build your own small off-grid home solar system, step by step. So, please stay tuned for that amazing course.

Now, if you have been thinking about installing a solar system in your home and haven't yet decided on what kind of system you want to go with for a permanent installation, maybe you might consider thinking of a small yet portable solar generator. When considering a smaller solar generator, there are definitely many different ways you can go, and there are literally tons of options out there. I just bought myself a complete solar package recently called the Jackery 2000, and it also comes with 4/200-Watt Solar Panels to charge the system with. I plan on using it while working at my property in the mountains to charge my cordless tools, cell phone, laptop, string lights, coffee pot, etc, instead of having to constantly run my generator all the time. Don't get me wrong, I am totally glad that I have my gas generator to use for backup power, but I know having this new portable solar system is going to make things a lot easier and more convenient for me. Once I can get the small new cabin finished on the property, It will also be a relief to be able to use the Jackery for many other things whenever I start staying at the property more and more. Being able to use the Jackery is also going to be a huge benefit while I am working on sizing up the actual solar system that will be installed at the cabin.

I know a big question that most people wonder about solar generators is whether they really work. Well, Solar Generators have definitely come a long way. They can provide lots of off-grid energy consistently and over extended periods of time without requiring anything other than the power of the sun. Today's solar generators provide a green solution for power generation that, in many cases, can be as effective or even more effective than propane or gas-powered generators, and basically, after the up-front cost of the equipment, solar generators have no additional running expenses compared their gasoline-powered generator counterparts and also means that you won't have to listen to that sound of a motor running all night keeping you awake while trying to relax while on your weekend get-a-way. They provide an unlimited energy source from direct sunlight, so there is no need to buy any fuel, which means you won't have to worry about carrying any extra gas cans that could spill over to cause a stinky hazardous mess and with no moving parts, means less maintenance costs to worry about. I know that the solar generator market is booming right now. Many people are ecstatic to be able to use these petroleum-free units in so many different places. I do not have a favorite model, and I do not receive any kind of payment or compensation for referring to any of these products. However, I would still like to share these resources with you so you can check them out for yourself and see what you might think of these amazing products.

www.renogy.com

www.jackery.com

www.4patriots.com

www.bluettipower.com

www.naturesgenerator.com

www.oupes.com

www.hysolis.com

SUMMARY
INSIGHTS TO BUILDING OFF-GRID

I would like you to think about all of the different things we have been over in this book. We have really covered a lot of ground in the short amount of time that we have had to cover the material involved in building a small off-grid home. First, we identified that there are a lot of people in the world today who are growing ever so tired of living in the everyday Rat-Race and dealing with all of the different self-imposed problems that our society is gradually forcing us to live with. These people do not agree with how the world is rapidly changing and have had their eyes opened in many different ways over the past few years by the unwanted changes and newly fabricated rules that are continually being imposed upon them... they have a hunger for doing their own thing and this particular group of people are unique in their own way and don't want to follow the crowd. They are continually looking for different ways to detach themselves and their families from all of the unsettling craziness that is growing around them. This group of people is in search of a more peaceful and simpler lifestyle, and for the most part, they just want to be left alone. This group of people has started saving their money, working on gathering up their resources, cashing in on their retirement funds, educating themselves about off-grid living, buying suitable land, building an off-grid home, water collection, solar power, homesteading, gardening, canning, raising chickens, raising ducks, raising goats and other livestock, prepping, survivalism and just about anything that has to do with being self-sustainable in some form or another and they are constantly doing research on how they can make this all become a possibility for themselves. You may have been a little overwhelmed or even slightly confused about what to do or where to start first or simply not have known which direction to turn in order to get yourself started. We then touched base on looking at what to do by putting together a plan for yourself. Identifying what is involved in creating your plan. Take a look into your finances and see what kind of budget you have to work with, and if you aren't where you want to be, then identify how you are going to come up with the money you are going to need to execute your plan. After your budget, you'll need to start looking into the land. Is it going to be closer to or farther away from the city? Different places you can look for land, and knowing that the farther your land is going to be from a major city or municipality, the easier it will be to secure the land and build your small off-grid home. Once you find a potential piece of property, you will need to know what questions to ask, such as about planning and zoning rules in the area where you want to buy your land and build your small off-grid home on to make sure it is ok to follow through with your plans to build there. If not there, how can you look for unrestricted land so you can build the home you want to build? I also introduced you to 3 different types of structures that you could consider building on your land. The 1st Type of home suggested was an Earthbag Structure. The earthbag Structure has been around for centuries and has some amazing thermal mass properties to help with your home's efficiency. An Earthbag Home is super cheap to build; however, the main drawback to this method of construction is that it is very labor-intensive. The second type of building that I suggest building is a DIY Aircrete Structure. Although Aircrete (or Cellular Concrete) as it is known in the commercial industry, has been used to build many structures in Europe over the past several years, it is now gaining a lot of popularity in the DIY sector because it is also cheap to build with and is much less labor intensive to build with than the previous construction method. It has recently gained a tremendous amount of popularity because of its ease to make as well as its lightweight and super-insulative characteristics. Last but not least, the Third Type of building that I mentioned was the shed-to-home conversion. This is merely purchasing a pre-built or build yourself a small shed and converting it to your own small off-grid home. There are many different manufacturing companies to choose from depending on what part of the world you live in. There are many manufacturers today that will sell you anything from a raw shell of the shed to a fully completed home, built to your personal specifications, delivered and set-up on your land. Now, this would add a considerable cost to your project, but it would enable you to be able to move into your land much faster and without all the hassle of building your own home. Now for me personally, I would rather build my own home instead of having to spend that large of a chunk of money upfront, but I had to mention it simply because it is an option, if you had the money to invest. Which would still be cheaper than having a huge home built in a regular neighborhood somewhere. Deciding to build your own shed and convert it into your own small off-grid home would not only save you a lot of money in the long run, but it would also allow you to build the kind of structure that you wanted as opposed to having to settle for a manufacturers' particular design that you may not really want to settle with. However, that choice is definitely yours to make and once you have decided on what type of structure you want for your home there are now different things you are going to have to take into consideration when preparing your land to build your home on, such as how to look at the land and notice how the drainage will be across your property so your home won't flood whenever there is a big rainstorm. We discussed how to orient your home on the property for prevailing winds and orientating for the rise and sunset of the sun so the primary sun through the day isn't continually heating up a large picture window you may want to install in your living room area because you're going to want the inside temperature of your home to be as comfortable as possible. Taking these things into consideration now will definitely save you some unwanted frustration later down the road. I know whenever I was working on building the domes for the monastery this was one of my favorite things to do. Laying out the building design and taking into consideration of the prevailing winds, how the sun came up in the east and set in the west... I never knew how important these little things would be to when it came to actually building the structures and once, they were built and to be able to actually feel the change in air temperature as soon as I came in from the outside heat into the coolness of the inside of the domes...and there wasn't any air-conditioning or anything, just the natural coolness of the air. Words couldn't describe the feeling. It was just amazing. Another system we covered for our small off-grid home was Rainwater Collection. We discussed some different types of containers we can use to collect rainwater, as well as how to treat our tanks to keep them clean and from being able to grow algae and bacteria. We also discussed some different options we could use for our own personal drinking water systems that we could easily keep on the table or on the counter in our kitchens so we could have safe clean water to drink whenever we wanted. There were Three different types of DIY Septic Systems that we went over so we could safely be able to treat the solid waste that was produced from our homes. We covered the basic composting toilet, which is the simplest system we could put together. Next we covered the 2-

Barrel System which is buried outside of our home and could easily support the waste of two people and lastly we covered the Vermicomposting System that uses earthworms to speed up the composting process and is becoming a more and more acceptable way to treat and process solid waste than the normal flush septic waste systems currently used by most people and government body's that treat and process solid waste around the world today. One of the main things that our home simply cannot be without is power. Our homes require power or some form of electricity in order to make it comfortable for us to live in, so we do not have to feel like we are giving up one of our largest luxuries. There are different forms of power available, but we need our home to be independent, so it will be a true off-grid home. Yes, the government will offer us Solar Programs and try to make us feel as if we are free from being dependent on the Power Grid... The problem with these systems is that they are Grid -Tied Systems... So, whenever the power goes out in your area... Guess What? Your power goes out too. Because you are tied to the regular power grid. The only thing your system does is feed power back to the power grid whenever the power is on... Thus, feeding the system power back... making money for them... But they will make you feel as if you are getting real service from this. Another is that you buy a system... And instead of paying an electric bill, you are paying for a \$20,000 to \$40,000 Solar System over time... So, you will still be paying a monthly bill to somebody and if you decide to sell your house and move it stays with the home and it's a loan that you still have to pay off and it feeds back into the system. So, the only way you can truly benefit from having solar hooked to your home, is to have your own system. Yes, there is an initial layout, as there is with everything, but once you purchase it, the power you use from your system benefits you and your home. No Strings Attached. Solar companies will argue the points I have made, so I suggest you investigate this and see for yourself. Of course, this is just my take on things. You will need to take into account what appliances you are going to be using in your home and then size your solar system accordingly. Assembling your own system can definitely be done for a fraction of the cost of what most commercial companies will charge you. Last but not least, if you don't need a large system, there are many different companies out there that sell portable solar generators. These are a great option if you only need to power up some basic things in your cabin. They come with their own solar panels to recharge, and you just plug them in wherever you need to have power. Some even have added on battery systems that you can just add on additional power packs to make your system larger so it will last longer and support more power usage, the only limitation is your budget, but you can purchase some very nice solar generator packages at a very reasonable cost.

Now that you have read through the process and now have a better vision of what all is involved in building your own Off-Grid Self-Sufficient Small Home. Let's go over a few key points that may indicate that you are ready to move forward with your dream of moving to an Off-Grid Property and Finally Building Your Own Off-Grid Self-Sufficient Style Home:

- You're a Do It Yourselfer that isn't afraid to get your hands dirty.
- You have been collecting different tools, reading books and materials to help you understand the work you need to be able to do once you get yourself moved to your off-grid property.
- You constantly watch videos and read books trying to learn as much as you can. You Subscribe to anyone's videos on You Tube and any other social media platforms where you think they may offer content on what can help you figure out how to get yourself set up in an off-grid lifestyle and you have notebook after

notebook filled with notes you have been writing down so you can always be able to reference the things you are wanting to do.

- You have bought Online Courses that you hope to gain knowledge from that will help teach you tips, tricks, and techniques to achieving your off-grid living dream.
- You are open to different building methods and are looking for alternative ways to build your off-grid self-sufficient style home.
- You realize that in order to have a certain kind of lifestyle you have to "Open Your Mind" and be willing to think "Outside-the-Box" and know that Everything can't always be done conventionally.
- You have to realize that this lifestyle isn't for everyone.
- You have to realize that it is going to take Hard Work, Sacrifice and Dedication to get you to where you want to be with Your Own Off-Grid Self-Sufficient Small Home and Lifestyle.

Now in summary, this book... by no means... is meant to be a step-by-step guide, however it is a very detailed comprehensive guide that that breaks down almost every aspect of what is involved in building your own off-grid small home. This book is mainly intended to help to open your eyes to some of the many different things that are involved to be able to start separating yourself from the chaos and confusion of what life has ultimately become for most everyone who may be looking for a way to change their lives. Many people think about buying land and building their own small off-grid home every day, and many people dream of buying land and building their own small off-grid home every day, but here is the Million Dollar question: Are YOU indeed ready for this? Regardless of what you may decide to do. The days will pass you by anyway. Will you continue to live in your current situation, or are you ready to take the leap and change the outcome of your life? You may be asking yourself, is it worth it? In my personal opinion... I will have to say, YES. We are all losing more of our freedoms every single day, not to mention the lawmakers, politicians, etc. are continuing to limit our access to things that should be easy to get every chance they get.

I would like to add this very important note of caution that you must be aware of and fully understand before embarking on this journey. You must understand that some of the methods and designs for building an alternative style building and lifestyle may not align with Some City, County, and State Code Ordinances and that you have to be willing to do whatever is needed in order to make your Personal Off-Grid Dreams become a reality. This means doing your own due diligence and understanding that a majority of Off-Grid homes will not be able to be financed through a bank or any other conventional means of financing as you would normally do as if you were building a regular home through a contractor or home builder. This is why I have laid out the steps in this book for you to start off with first thinking about building a small room about the size of a large master bedroom, then finishing it out and then adding on other rooms from there. That way you will be able to afford your new home without having to go into debt or obtain any financing for your home. And as I stated earlier, what will make this journey entirely worth it, is that your home will be TOTALLY PAID FOR Once You are Finished with it!!! Take the first step and just get started. You'll be surprised how easy it really is.

There are people every day that decide they have had enough and take their first step towards making a plan, purchasing their land, and moving themselves forward towards a better life, so they can get away from all the hustle and bustle of the daily rat race. Many people succeed and are Very Happy with their choices and wouldn't trade their new Off-Grid Self-Sustainable Lifestyle for anything in the world. However, there are people that go out to start a new life and they end up struggling more and have to throw in the towel on their dreams because they were not fully prepared for what they were going to encounter once they set off on their new journey or they will start to have doubt in themselves and others will pick up on this and try to talk you out of your dreams.

<u>DO NOT</u> Allow the Dream-Steelers to take this away from you!!!

<u>Fight For it</u>!!!

<u>THIS IS YOUR TIME</u>!!!

DESCRIPTION

Wanna Move Off-Grid? It May Be Easier Than You Think...

Here are just a few things you are going to discover:

--Finding and Buying Land --Assessing Your Property --How to Layout and Orient for Your Structures --Designing and Building Your Home (I Give You 3 Different Examples of Structures for You to Consider to Help You Keep Your Ideas Flowing)

--<u>The 3 Main Systems</u> That You Will Need to Make Your Off-Grid Home Self-Sustainable. * Simple Solar System (I Give You Different Examples) Also How to Calculate How Big Your System Needs to Be. * Water Catchment System (I Give You Different Examples) What You Need to do to Have a Pressurized Water System. (It's Easier Than You Think) * DIY Septic Systems, For Waste Management (I Give You 3 Different Examples)

–<u>The 3 Additional Things</u> That You Can Add to Make Your Home Even More Comfortable, As Well. *Water Filtration Systems (Different Examples) *Hot Water (Example) What You Need to do to Have On-Demand Hot Water (We All Love Hot Showers) *Mini-Split A/C and Heating Unit (Yes, You Can Also Have Air Conditioning... If You Do the Right Calculations When You Size Up Your Solar System)

*And So Much More...